MW00666871

DANCING WITH THE UNIVERSE

The Makings of a Medium

June Edward

"The Massachusetts Medium"

Thriving, Not Just Surviving Through Dysfunction.

FORWARD

My father knew I would write a book, someday and tell the family secret. I remember him asking me, on many occasions not to write my book until he was dead. He passed December 21, 2017.

My oldest sister Linda, my youngest brother Albert, and I, were the only three strong enough in our family to make it through. Although none of us are perfect, or unscathed, we were able to understand there was a problem, that our lives weren't normal, and do our best to change as adults.

I've always been a very psychic person. But it was only recently that I realized I have always been a medium as well. As a child, I would hear voices, and talk to people, that didn't seem to be there. It was kind of like not knowing that you're a really good basketball player, because you only threw the ball a few times and never really applied yourself to the sport. But once I was ready, and I asked the angels to open me up, it was like the flood gates had swung wide open! Many things have happened to me that may have enhanced my abilities. I don't really know. It's possible that it was just the grand plan for me (we all have one)! There are no accidents in life, everything happens for a reason, and at the right time.

I'm telling my story so that other people can understand that they can overcome their upbringing. There are things that happen to you, and mistakes that you make, but it doesn't mean that's who you are. No one is perfect. You make the best decisions you can at the time, and you learn as you go. You can rise above the damage done to you, heal, and heal others. My hope is that more abuse and dysfunction is out in the open, the less will occur, and the less people will feel stigmatized. We're all a little damaged one way or the other. You can overcome and not let the negative things that happen in life define you. Although I feel my best years are still ahead, this is my journey.

Millie

This book is dedicated to my sister Millie. Since your passing you have been an amazing guide for me in the spirit world. You've shown me insights and given me knowledge I otherwise wouldn't have. You were an earth angel here, more a mother to me than a sister, and an amazing master on the other side, proof that love never dies.

CONTENTS

THE BEGINNING

I was born in 1963 with parents that were already getting on in years. They grew up during the depression, with parents that did not know how to express love to their children. Apparently, a lot of people from the depression era learned to never throw anything out either! I lived in a hoarding house growing up, with two mentally ill parents, that were verbally, physically, and sexually abusive. I am one of eight children, five girls and three boys. The children, in order from oldest to youngest, are Linda, Gwen, Arthur, Millie, myself, June, Shirley, William, and the youngest, Albert. When a family has that many children, I don't believe you can raise them. I liken it more to being dragged up by each other! It's also very difficult to have a relationship with all the other siblings, since there are large gaps in ages. I can only remember my parents being "old". They never went out and played with us, or took us to the beach, or interacted with us in any "fun" way. I can never remember either of my parents telling me they loved me as a child, or giving me a hug. It was just chaos every day and going through the motions to try and survive from one day to the next. My oldest sister tells me that there was a time when my mother kept a clean house, and things weren't so crazy. Apparently it was prior to having so many children.

When I started writing this book, both parents were still here on the earth plane. My father was 93 years old, on his deathbed, and doing his best to try and destroy what he could of the three children that made a life for themselves and survived. My father had been one of the first Mr. Donut franchise owners in the country. My mother was 92, in a nursing home, and extremely grateful that I rescued her from the bug-infested, drug-haven apartment complex she had been living in. Most of my knowledge about earlier family life came from my mom. No one was allowed near my dying father, except for my younger brother William, and his son William Jr., who had both taken steps to relieve him of any money or property he still had. Unfortunately, some of the laws that are made to protect us are so strict that in the end, they end up harming the people they are supposed to protect. William and his son even forged my father's signature on a new will. We could have disputed the will but in the time it would have taken for the case to meander its way through the courts, while we paid thousands of dollars to attorneys, the money would have been gone. My father passed on December 21, 2017. This is where trust and faith come in. I trust in the Universe, that there is a God that sees all, and that Karma will do her job. Somehow they will be punished for what they did, if not here than in the next life.

When you're a child growing up in dysfunction and abuse, and this is what you see and feel, you don’t know any different. Only as an adult, if you're not too damaged, are you able to change the way you live and learn to treat other people in the world around you differently than the way you learned growing up. It can be a challenge not to perpetuate the dysfunction, since children learn what they live. By the grace of God, you don’t want to pass the damage onto your own children, or to continue the cycle. No one is perfect, myself included. We can only do the best we can with the tools that we have at any given moment, and hope to be and do better tomorrow than we did today.

The story I'm about tell you is true. It may seem a little bizarre to some of you, but others may connect to the things that happened to me. I have found in my lifetime that everyone has a struggle of some sort whether emotional or physical, abundance or lack. It's the old adage; sometimes bad things happen to good people. Believe it or not, we chose this journey before we arrived here. We chose our parents, we chose our siblings, and we chose the lessons that we wanted to learn or teach while we are here. Sometimes if we remember that, and look for the lesson, it makes life just a little bit easier when the times get tough.

THE FAMILY

My oldest sister Linda and I are ten years apart, and we have been fortunate enough to have a decent relationship with each other, although even that has gone back and forth through the years. I remember when I was young, and she moved out of the house and got a job working for The Providence Journal in Rhode Island. I used to watch the Mary Tyler Moore Show, and thought that my sister must have been just like her. When she got married at eighteen, I was eight years old. I remember my mother shipping me off to stay the night at a stranger's house, so that I could be the flower girl at a wedding. Only recently did I discover that it was actually my sister's wedding. I never put the two together, and I didn't really know my sister then. I remember the ring bearer telling me not to drink the toast, because it was wine. I thought that he must be mistaken, because they wouldn't give wine to children, so I drank it. I remember it burned my throat. I guess they do give wine to kids! But by the time I turned sixteen, my sister and I were best of friends. Though like any sisters, have had our trials and tribulations through the years. She moved away from the area where the family lives to Florida more than twenty years ago. She has a husband who is a few years older than she is and one son.

The next oldest sibling is Gwen. When I was ten years old, I received a phone call from someone asking to speak with me. It was a man from a collection agency. Apparently, my sister Gwen had stolen my identity, and used it to obtain credit. I really didn't have much to do with her after that. The only exception was when she had her first child. She was involved with the Hare Krishna cult at the time, and had gotten pregnant by a man that was married and twice her age. She originally named my niece Lakshmana, but when Lakshmana hit school age, all the kids were teasing her about her nick name, Lucky! She then legally changed her name to Katie. Gwen suffered from manic depression, and ended up having a manic episode, after the baby was born. She was institutionalized in Virginia and the baby was put into foster care there. My father had her brought to a local hospital close to the family and I took care of the newborn baby that summer I was ten. Manic depression runs through the family, and only me, my oldest sister and youngest brother seemed to have escaped it. Apparently, it's brought on by drugs or alcohol at an early age, and we, by the grace of God, avoided it. Gwen had also been very much abused as a child. I remember seeing all of her school pictures; she had dark circles under her eyes, because she never slept. She's always been a "poor thing". Obviously a very sensitive child, she kept trying to get her father's love and attention into adulthood. When she threatened to expose him as an adult, not necessarily knowing he was still abusing the other siblings, he cut her off from his life, and refused to ever speak to her again. They didn't speak for almost forty years, basically until he was on his deathbed.

The next oldest sibling is my brother Arthur. He got involved in drugs and alcohol at an early age. I can remember telling my mother I saw him smoking at church when I was only seven. My parents ended up sending him to a prestigious private high school, Thayer Academy, in the footsteps of my oldest sister Linda. It's now an even more exclusive prep school. He was expelled, for dealing drugs. After that, my mother tells me that he got in some trouble after having sex with a girl about the age of seventeen, and was upset with my mother because when he got home late the door to the house had been locked. She said he found one of my father's handguns, and held it to her head to threaten her. Years later he would break into the family home to steal items, and arranged to have a brand new vehicle stolen that my father had bought for the business. As much as I tried to have a relationship with my brother when we got older, he ended up marrying a controlling, mentally and physically impaired woman who encouraged his dysfunctional and narcissistic behavior. When the two of them moved in together, she was on welfare, and she thought she found the golden goose! She sent her son to go live with his father, saying that she didn't think it was right for my brother to support him financially since it wasn't his child. They came into money, when my brother, the president of the Bottle Club, sold the highest priced bottle of its kind ever recorded. When my younger sister died, he came to her house as I was cataloging and removing her belongings, to see what he could take of hers. My father asked if I would be the executor of her estate, since he was too old to do it properly Arthur had been watching the house for weeks, knowing that I was coming with a moving crew to take out her belongings. He then told me not to take any of her boyfriend's things. I didn't talk to him for years, after he caused a problem with his wife at my wedding, and he got upset that I spilled his marijuana addiction to the doctors during my sister Shirley's treatment, and explaining the family history. The only blessing is that he didn't bring any children into the world to be raised into his dysfunction.

The next older sibling that I also had a good relationship with as an adult was my sister Millie. She ran away from home at the age of fifteen, to live in a Hare Krishna Temple in Boston. She basically ran away from the severe dysfunction and tried to save herself. My understanding is that she was one of the most abused in the family. My oldest sister Linda walked in on my father on top of her when she was only around twelve or thirteen years old. Sadly, she went from one violent abusive situation to another. The Hare Krishna's sent her from state to state to hide her from my father, and basically brainwashed her with lack of sleep and food. She had been forcibly raped many times, and then they married her off to two different men within the religion. The first one abused her so badly, and beat her so severely, that the elders declared the marriage null and void, and married her off to someone else. She was allowed to stay at the temple as long as she was able to sell books and pan handle money. Once she became pregnant however, and wasn't able to carry the books with the baby, they threw her out. She did stay married to this man until she died, and although he was a drug addict and cheated on her regularly, they had six children together. She moved to California, and lived on the edge of the Sequoia National Forest in an area where other Hare Krishna people lived in a commune of sorts. My dad sent her money through the years to help her buy some land and build a house.

Not having any child rearing skills however, as soon as the kids were old enough, she would field them out to other families within the religion to raise them. She has had two children actually make it in life on their own, and the other four are mentally ill and dysfunctional. My sister died at the age of fifty- three of cervical cancer. She went to a male doctor that was threatening to her, and he scared her so much she didn't go back. By the time she did, the cancer was stage four, and had eaten through her bladder and other organs. My brother Albert and I flew out to see her, since she was only given a few weeks to live.

During her time here, she formed a non-profit soup kitchen that she would cook for every day in her apartment, and bring to Venice Beach to feed the homeless. She was a kind and loving person, and wanted to make the world a better place. I am blessed to have her as a guide now on the other side, and she is with me daily.

I am the next in line, and then my sister Shirley. She and I were very close as small children. We were less than a year apart, and shared a bedroom together until the age of ten. She was also very close to my sister Millie, and when they played together they always excluded me. Years later, my sister Millie said she never realized she was doing that, but she always felt she had a special bond with my sister Shirley. They spend a lot of time together on the other side. I remember when Shirley got to be about ten years old, she became a real tomboy. It was after we moved to South Attleboro. She was an angry child, and always defiant of any authority. I was so busy with my own life, and trying to survive, that I didn't notice that my father had made her the next target of his abuse! For that reason, she turned at an early age to drugs and alcohol.

I remember she was found by a neighbor passed out in a snowbank during the blizzard of 1978. She was thirteen at the time, and had to go to the hospital to have her stomach pumped due to her alcohol level. I slept through the ambulance and the commotion, because I always went to bed at 10 o'clock. As time went on, she figured out that she could get anything she wanted from my father; all she had to do is threaten to expose him to the authorities! He bought her numerous cars, expensive jewelry, a house, and supported her to the tune of about a hundred and fifty thousand dollars per year. She never went past the ninth grade, and never had more than a waitressing job.

She had a manic episode at about the age of thirty, and went on a high-speed chase with the police. She was driving on four rims, because she had hit every curb and blown every tire. The police had to smash out the window of the car to remove her. She clearly wanted to die. It wasn't the first time. She had no less then fourteen serious car accidents while under the influence, and almost lost an eye at one point. She also got into a physical altercation with a previous boyfriend and stabbed him in the chest with a kitchen knife. If it hadn't been for the news station interviewing the neighbors, who always heard the fighting, she probably would have gone to jail for attempted murder.

The laws being what they were, they were going to just keep releasing her from mental institutions until she killed herself, unless someone stepped in. No one else in the family wanted anything to do with helping her, including my father. I offered to be her legal guardian to make sure she got some help. There for the grace of God go I. It could have just as easily have been me and not her. She hated me for it while she was here. She didn't like the fact that she didn't have 100% control over her own decisions, and that she had to be injected monthly with medication, to keep her stable enough to take her oral medications daily. She would only contact me for help when she needed help getting out of some illegal scam she pulled, or when she needed her current boyfriend removed from the house.

The last boyfriend she had was sponging off of her for years. He knew that my father paid for everything, so he basically lived for free. He had a bit of a gambling habit, and he would take Shirley with him when he went to the local casino. He had multiple sclerosis, but it didn't stop him from doing any of his daily routine. He smoked and drank, and worked under the table, and although he knew Shirley wasn't supposed to drink on her medication, he would encourage her to do so anyway. Shirley asked me to throw him out at one point, but then let him move back because she was lonely. He was apparently having an affair prior to my sister's passing, with our niece Katie, one of Gwen's daughters. The two of them were stealing Shirley's jewelry, and selling it to the local pawn shop. Shirley had thousands of dollars' worth of gold chains. My brother Albert had put hooks in her closet to hang them all across the back wall. I believe Katie and her boyfriend Dennis were afraid Shirley was going to discover what was going on, so he took the opportunity to overmedicate her with his prescription medication. It was the only medication found during the autopsy. It took him two days, and she died in her bed at the age of forty- seven. I located the pawn ticket to the only piece of jewelry that was recovered after her death, in the possession of my niece, Katie. Sadly, the police refused to investigate, since they saw it as one more problematic person gone.

Then there is William. He is the next one younger than me. He was abused by the other brothers and sisters, as well as the neighborhood kids. Being only seven when he was torn away from the home he knew, he took it really hard. My older sister Millie and brother Arthur used to put him in a closet for hours if he didn't behave. The neighborhood kids would make fun of him and beat him up, and call him a sissy. He grew up to be an angry, dangerous sociopath, an alcoholic and addicted to drugs. My father never paid any attention to him, or any of us for that matter, unless it was out of guilt. When William got into high school, he started doing steroids, and joined the football team. He also started lifting weights. He became a force to contend with.

He raped a girl that he went to high school with. When the girl's family called the police, my father protected him and denied it. Since my father had one of the most lucrative businesses in town, he held a lot of political power. Then my brother started threatening the girl and intimidating her and her family. The family moved out of the town within a few months.

He then set his sights on me! I was cleaning the fish tanks that I had in the living room one Sunday afternoon. He came up behind me with a knife threatening to kill me. I was seventeen. I moved out, into an apartment with a guy I had dated for a few weeks, to get away from him.

He was married for a short time, and he was physically and verbally abusive to his wife. They had one child together, and my brother was just as abusive with the baby. My father bought them a brand-new mobile home, in one of the local mobile parks. My brother continued to drink and do drugs and he was fired from several jobs he held as a machinist, for fighting with co-workers. My brother Albert had gone to his house a few times to intervene in situations with my father, and on one occasion, William fired a shot gun at him, missing, and put a hole in the floor of his mobile home.

It was no surprise that his wife finally left. She married a police officer and moved to Florida, so William would have to leave her alone. My father wanted my brother to have custody of the baby however, because he was the only male to carry on the family name. He paid her a sum of money, she agreed to the name change, and William Jr. went to live with my sociopathic brother! Guess what he raised? A more dangerous sociopathic child! My father took pride in teaching him how to pick locks, and encouraged him to live a criminal lifestyle. He was sent to the training school at around ten, and by fifteen, never went back to school again! My father would brag and tell everyone the kid was a genius, when in reality, he's a dangerous sociopath.

My father supported the two of them to the tune of about two hundred thousand dollars a year. He bought them numerous vehicles, and would deposit large sums of money into the checking account for them to have spending money and play the stock market. They also were big into dealing and using drugs. When they stabbed two people in the middle of the night when a drug deal went bad, he moved them out of Rhode Island and into his second wifes' home in Massachusetts during the night, to protect them from the police. They both, through the years, were physically and verbally abusive to my father. If he said he didn't have the money to give them, they would push him, and call him an old man, and tell him he better get the money! So he continued to feed them large sums of money, and refused to let me or my youngest brother intervene with the police.

At one point in time we decided to have my brother Albert get a restraining order against William Jr, to keep him away from my father and the business, because he had taken over my father's apartment, and was selling drugs out of the business. When Albert was out of the country having surgery, my father went to court and had the restraining order dropped! He created a nightmare with William and William Jr. In his later years, he lived that nightmare. Unfortunately, they destroyed his business and stole everything he owned, so the rest of the family got nothing in the end. They literally held him hostage on his deathbed and wouldn't allow the family to see him. Karma, baby Karma, she's a bitch. Eventually, I expect them to both end up in prison for something. It's just a matter of time.

My youngest brother, Albert, is five years younger than me. There is a fifteen- year age gap between him and my oldest sister, Linda. As much as she has tried to connect with him he has told me, he doesn't really know her and feels quite distant. Since I was in the middle, I'm lucky enough to have a good relationship with my youngest brother

Albert as well as my oldest sister. When he turned sixteen, my father bought him a car. It seems he bought multiple cars for all the kids in the family, except for me.

I was the black sheep of the family. I was told when I was ten that I didn't get any Christmas presents, because I didn't ask for anything. Meanwhile my younger sister Shirley received a long leather jacket, matching boots, and a leather pocketbook. (She ran away to New York shortly after to find our sister Millie, and sold them on the street to buy food). I didn't believe that should be how it worked, so I refused to ask for anything ever! Years later, it became a problem for me to accept anything from anyone, especially a partner. It took me years to get over this.

Anyway, right after getting the car, Albert got into a car accident coming home from school. Someone cut him off when they were pulling out of a gas station, and he tried to brake on sand. He was, however, driving quite fast; the speed limit at that time was fifty miles per hour. He hit the metal pole that held the gas station sign. The car was small, and he would have died if he hadn't slid under the dash somehow from the impact. At the time, I had been married to my first husband for about three or four months. I received a phone call from Shirley. Sadly, being dysfunctional, she always had difficulty with priorities. She didn't call to tell me my brother had an accident, and they didn't think he was going to make it, she called to see if I could cover her shift at my father's donut shop so she could go to the hospital! I hadn't worked for my father at that point in over a year.

I lost it emotionally! As much as my brother was young and doesn't really remember, I was the one that toilet trained him when he was five years old. I watched over him like he was my own child when he was little. My husband at the time drove me to the hospital. I was only allowed to see him briefly as they took him into surgery. He had a broken neck, as well as other major injuries. They didn't know if he might end up permanently paralyzed. They removed his spleen, and put rods in his ankle, and drilled holes in his head to stabilize him in a halo. They also wired his jaw shut, and he lost most of his teeth. The only good thing was that he was alive!

He's told me recently, that he had a near death experience that day. He remembers being out of his body and watching them remove him from the car. He didn't go to heaven though. He didn't talk to anyone or see any angels. I think his soul just left his body for a short time. This happens a lot with people, even when they're sleeping. As long as the body stays alive, they can return. If the body dies however, they obviously can't go back, and would need to go into the light. He ended up recuperating at our brother Arthur's house with his crazy wife. But that's a story only he can share!

Albert took a year to fully recover and walk again. He never returned to high school. He took his GED and went to work beside my father in the family business. This is where he stayed until my father's death, and the closing of the business. He met a lovely woman that became his second wife a few years ago, and they live part of the time in Florida and part of the time in Columbia. His first wife went to school with me growing up and is a horrible person. She actually tried to kill my brother with rat poison, when he was trying to divorce her. If he hadn't moved out she may have succeeded!

WHERE IT ALL STARTED

My mother was born in Chicago, Illinois. She always felt like she didn't fit in with her family. She had one brother and one sister, but her mother always treated her differently. It is evident that she never received much love from anyone in her family, since she’s always had difficulty expressing, love and affection. I can’t remember either of my parents ever giving me a hug or telling me they loved me as a child. I do know that she loves each and every one of her children. At 92, she's finally able to tell us. We all have free will, so even though we've chosen this life, our parents, and our children, things can change based on the decisions that we make. As my mom lies in her nursing home bed, and reflects upon her life, I know this is not how she expected to live hers.

She grew up believing that her aunt was her mother, and that her father was really her uncle. Back in those days, if you weren’t put up for adoption, families tried to give you to someone else in the family. She now believes that her mother was the butcher's daughter that lived across the street from her growing up. She was brought up calling her real father “uncle”. She only actually saw her mother a couple of times, and the woman tried to hide from my mom when that happened. My mother's father (not her real father, but the one she had known as her father), died when she was seventeen. He worked for the railroad company and had somehow injured his leg. A few years later he apparently developed a blood clot that went to his lung. My mother received a message at school to come home right away, that her dad was not doing well. She was able to make it home in time, and she was able to say goodbye to him as he passed in the bed.

Shortly after her father's death, her sister went with her to the local USO show. My father happened to be stationed at the local navy base, and was also at the USO show. She tells me that both she and her sister were flirting with him, and they had asked him if he would give them the scarf off of his uniform. Within a week they received two scarves in the mail, one for each. From that point on, they my mother and father dated, all through the spring, and were married that summer. She said they really only went out a few times. One date was a canoe ride on the local pond. She said her sister and my dad put the boat away but took a very long time coming back. I ran across a picture of them all out on the pond that day when we were cleaning out the house we all lived in, prior to demolition. My mother was a stunningly beautiful when she was young.

My mom had been working as a telegraph delivery girl at the time, delivering messages while on roller-skates! When she told her mother that she was going to city hall to marry my dad, her mother informed her that she didn’t approve, and that it wouldn't be happening if her father had still been alive. Apparently she was not a fan of her getting married so young. Although she was a year younger than my dad, (according to her birth certificate), in Massachusetts, where my father was from, he had to have written permission from his mother since he was under twenty- one years old.

My mom contends that she was always smarter than the kids in her grade, and that her birth certificate had been altered by a year, to cover up the fact that she had been adopted by her aunt. Back in those days, families tried to keep things under wraps, and as quiet as possible,

My mother's sister was moving out west to Arizona, and my mom got out of work early to come home and say goodbye to her. When she arrived, she found my father there and her sister already gone! He had already taken her to the train station, and she wasn't coming back. Right then my mother knew in her gut, that he had slept with her sister. She said even then, my father was all about sex, and she told him she wouldn't sleep with him until they were married! My mother told me that one of the first leaves that my father had from the service, he drove across the country to go see her sister. She believes he found out she was pregnant. My mother never spoke to her sister again, since they didn't have phones in those days, and she never saw her again. Her sister, my aunt, died in her forties of breast cancer. The question has always remained however, whether or not my cousin is really my half-sister.

Before my father got out of the military, and after they got married, my mother continued to live in Chicago. She came into a sum of money when her grandfather on her mother's side passed away. She took the money and invested in a three-family home. My mother was very intelligent, and was always good with money, unlike my father. When my father found out that she had done this, he became enraged. Apparently, he was upset that she would make a decision without him. He sold the house, and he didn't need her permission to do so since they were married. She has no idea how much money he received for it, because he would not tell her. He also did not put the money into any joint account that she would have access to. He basically just stole it!

My mom decided she wanted to go to college. But when she applied she found out she was missing a lot of the core courses that were required. Her high school apparently did not offer them back then. Therefore, she moved to Holbrook to live with my grandmother, my father's mother, and enrolled in the public high school there to take the courses she needed. After that, my father got out of the navy, and they moved to Connecticut. My father was able to go to college on the G.I. Bill. My mother had already enrolled in the University of Connecticut, but when my father decided to go, it was his decision that she needed to go back to work because they needed an income. She then took a job working in a medical laboratory, where she worked on a vaccine to prevent polio. She was never able to go back and finish college, since my father always found some other excuse why she couldn't. My father graduated with an engineering degree. Back in those days, the degree encompassed electrical engineering, mechanical, civil, and structural engineering. When he graduated, he took an engineering job in Virginia. My parents had been married at this point at least ten years, and still had no children.

Somehow, my father ended up getting a hernia. When he had the surgery to repair it, it corrected his infertility issue. Apparently, he had a condition called a vericoceles where a vein runs too close to the testicles, and heats the sperm up enough to kill it. As soon as they moved to Virginia, my mother became pregnant with my oldest sister Linda. My mother was a very independent woman, and had no problem doing things on her own. She told me she would load the baby in the backseat of the car, and drive all the way back to Holbrook Massachusetts many times. She had saved quite a bit of money working when my father was in college, and they used the money to buy a television set. They had left it at my grandmother's house prior to moving. She drove by herself with the baby, all the way to Massachusetts from Virginia to pick up the TV and bring it back, in winter!

She told me when they officially moved out of Virginia and they were heading back home to Holbrook, they barely made it through Worcester with a bad storm going on. The storm ended up being the first confirmed tornado touchdown in Massachusetts. I'm sure it must have been pretty scary!

My father was in the Naval Reserves for twenty years. Knowing that he was getting called back up for active duty service, to work as an engineer for the Korean War, he took a job working for a company selling windows and doors in Rochester, New York. They rented a fully furnished apartment, and at the time had just my sister Linda. But mom was pregnant with my sister Gwen. They weren't there very long and moved back to Holbrook for a short time. My mother's brother Alfred was also serving in the Korean War. My father also had an uncle that was the private photographer during the war for Bob Hope. He used to send her fine china pieces from Japan when he was traveling there. He sent mostly teacups and knick- knacks, but they would be very valuable antiques today.

I remember my dad telling stories of traveling back and forth from Pennsylvania quite often, and how dirty the city was from all the manufacturing. It used to be a glass manufacturing city, and the black soot would spew out of the chimneys from burning the coal. He said it was so dark that you couldn't see the sun during the day.

My mother tells me that in lieu of pay, my father would take windows and doors as payment. My grandmother had recently given both my father and my uncle a plot of land next to her own home, so that they could each build a house on it. They lived with my grandmother with Linda and the baby, Gwen, until they were able to finish building the house next door to her. My uncle Robert built his house next to my parents. My mother's mother died during this time. My mother refused to go to the funeral however, because she wasn't comfortable leaving the two children with her mother in law, and my father. In later years, it was always a bone of contention with my father. He claims she blamed him for not going, he says he should have insisted.

My mother tells me that my grandmother favored one child, my oldest cousin Martha, who was her first grandchild. My mother said that she couldn't be bothered with the rest of the kids. My oldest sister Linda confirms this as well. I only remember my grandmother coming to our house once to babysit. The house was fairly manageable at that time, and by manageable I mean you could walk from room to room still, without having to walk on the path that was about a foot deep of clothing and trash. There were still piles of clothing, books and newspapers everywhere, but the house was still livable. I remember she sat on the couch the whole time and didn't want to change a diaper on my baby brother Albert. I can recall that my mother got a diaper service when he was born, so she didn't have to wash all the diapers herself. Back then all you had were cloth diapers, and you could go through a hundred of those a day with a new baby!

We did go visit my grandmother at her house quite a few times. We would never really stay long though, and I don't ever remember ever eating there. Her kitchen was still from the 1930's, with an icebox for a refrigerator, and a hand pump on the kitchen sink. My dad ran across the bill for the remodel once, I know he planned on framing it, but I doubt that ever happened! I remember the total price was something like a hundred and twenty five dollars to renovate the whole kitchen. You would pay seven thousand dollars or more for that work today!

I remember she liked to preserve her vegetables in the fall, and had a root cellar. I can remember seeing a bunch of ball jars on the counter. I don't believe she had a garden, though. I had an uncle named Dick Hook that owned a farm that we would actually visit more often; I assume the vegetables came from him. The Hooks were my father's aunt and uncle, and they had two boys. My dad tells me the boys, (twins) were adopted. Back in the day, all adoptions went through the Catholic Church. The Hooks were older, and they weren't going to be able to adopt for that reason. They ended up adopting the twin boys, because they were premature, and no one else wanted them. They also weren't expected to live. Live they did! Other than some problems with eye sight, they grew up healthy, and are both still alive and in their eighties. Supposedly there is a connection with the Hook family and relatives coming over on the Mayflower. I remember one of my sisters had looked into joining the Mayflower girls once, and the requirement is to prove lineage.

When my grandmother got into her older years, she moved into my Uncle Robert and Ruth's house. Robert was my father's only sibling. They made a bedroom for her out of the front porch of the house. They found jars of wampum in the basement of her home when they moved her. Wampum is what the Indians used for money on the reservations; it's made from quahog shells. She kept them on the shelf next to her bed when she moved. My grandfather had some connection to the Indian tribe in Connecticut. I'm not really sure what the relationship was, but supposedly he had to have some Native American blood in him in order to spend time and gamble on the reservation. I did do quite a bit of my father's genealogy at one point in time, but the Bureau of Indian Affairs in Washington has been closed for many years due to lack of funding. In order to get information in Connecticut, you have to spend time at the museum. I did go up once, where I found a Fielding family that was very big in the Pequot tribe. My father has family members with that name, but I never got a chance to check further with my dad.

My father's father, my grandfather, also died young. He also worked on the railroad, the Providence to Worcester line. My father use to carry his gold watch that he was awarded for his service. It had a picture of my dad as a child with his dad, my grandfather. We used to have a lot of the train lamps hanging around the house when we were young as well. I was told he used to love to go fishing with his friends, and that's how we died, doing what he loved, fishing. He passed when my father was about eighteen.

My grandmother, my father's mother died when I was about nineteen years old, she was in her mid-eighties. I remember taking time off from work to go to the funeral. The minister that handled the service at the time was the cousin to one of the Smothers Brothers! They were a very famous comedy team that was on a television show when I was growing up. It was just a small service at the cemetery, and she was buried in a plain pine box. My father could not afford anything more and could not afford a headstone for her either. (Years later, we discover that he had been giving his money to some guy he knew that had a sob story to tell every week, a customer of his donut shop!) In later years, he purchased a huge stone monument made of a very rare rose quartz, and had everyone's names, birth and death dates put on it. When it was being made, the people that were engraving the stone spelled the last name wrong. They took it back to fix it, and my mother told me she was out driving one day and drove by a headstone on the side of the rode with her name on it! Talk about getting freaked out! She still talks about it today she was afraid it was an omen!

After the sales job my father had, he took a job as an engineer working for a company inventing things. He claimed he had a genius IQ, which I don't doubt. He invented many items and had them patented in four different countries. He holds patents in the United States, Canada, Japan, and Germany. He was extra proud of the German patent, since it was difficult to get, and his heritage is German. I know he invented the nozzle that blows the air out to open Wonder Bread bags on the assembly line. He developed the turn handle on the dispensers in the ladies and men's rooms, for condoms and tampons, and he invented the floating floor, that goes under main frame computers in high-rise buildings. This invention apparently has not been improved upon even today, and is still in use. He did not receive royalties however for these inventions, because he was in the employ of another company.

I can remember as a child, waiting in the drive through at a McDonalds, when he asked me to sign my name on a napkin. I asked him why, I was only about nine years old. He had just finished drawing an invention of a plumbing part on a napkin, and wanted it witnessed. Such a fine line between genius and insanity!

THE HOUSE ON MAPLEWOOD AVENUE

When my mother got pregnant with me, they decided they needed a larger home. They already had four children, and had converted the garage in the home into a bedroom. They bought a bungalow style split-level home, on Maplewood Avenue in the same town. My father being a structural engineer, decided to design and build the addition on the home himself. I suppose if he had applied himself, it might've been a good-looking home. Instead, it was an unfinished hot mess! I'm not sure at what point in time he started to put the addition on the house, I can remember living there as far back as three years old. I do not have any memory prior to that. My first bedroom that I can remember was actually the sunroom. It was called the sunroom for a reason; it was surrounded by windows and always very sunny! There were long heavy drapes covering the windows, and they had patterns in them that scared me. I could see faces in them. Nothing was decorated for children.

Apparently, I have always been very psychic, but I did not know that I was a medium as well. Many times I would be lying in bed in the morning, having been woken up by the sun, and hear someone call my name. Once or twice I got up, and ran into my parent's room to see if they were calling me. They were fast asleep. I would go back and pull the covers over my head, but a few times I could actually see the silhouette of someone leaning over the bed looking down at me. I found out in later years, that one of the previous owners died in that room and the other one died outside in the jalousie porch. I can only assume that was the shadow person I was seeing.

The house was huge by all standards. I would refer to it in later years as a mansion, especially to my own children. It had eight bedrooms, six bathrooms, two living rooms, a family room with a fireplace, the sunroom, a two- car attached and two-car detached garage, a heated driveway, two exterior jalousie porches, an office, a machine shop, and even a bomb shelter! Yes, my father built a concrete bomb shelter in the basement, just in case! He and my mother had lived through the war, and my dad fought in World War II. (As a child, they would make us take out the books in our lockers at school, and sit in the bottom when the air raid sirens would go off in town.) All told, I'd have to say the house alone was about 30000 square feet. It went on forever! Mind you, half of it was never finished. Some parts, more than others. Some rooms were just missing plaster, but other rooms were still just framed out. Three bathrooms just had framing and fixtures, no plumbing. The basements connected together but the attics of the houses did not. Imagine something that large filled almost floor to ceiling with clothing, books, newspapers, furniture, antiques, and any other miscellaneous item you could ever imagine! There was a huge back yard, partially fenced that we would play badminton over, and many out buildings, including another garage and what could be described as an apartment. There was also a machine shop with yet another garage. There was an old abandoned chicken coup that we used to play in, and about six acres of land that consisted of tall grass and lots of fruit trees.

My father had an office on one side of the basement, and started an engineering company of his own called Lincoln Controls. I can remember as a child, the phone would ring on the basement stairs all the time, and he would let us answer it! He never talked to anyone that called, though. I believe he just wanted the phone line to legitimize the business, to get a yellow page phone book listing. This was back in the day when you had phones with dials on them, and every time you picked up the phone an operator would come on the line. To call my grandmother, I would just tell the operator Randolph (which was the exchange) 9673. We even had party lines back then, where you share a phone line with another home, and have to wait for them to get off the line before you could call out. My dad had a very large machine shop in the back of the property, where he would manufacture items that he invented. He did receive royalties on those items, for twenty years each. As a kid I can remember him always tinkering back there. I also remember that he never repaired anything. Raccoons had gotten into the ceiling of the machine shop, and pulled down all the insulation. I believe he shot the raccoons, but never cleaned up the mess!

My Father the Pervert

From as far back as I can remember, my father would have inappropriate sexual conversations with all of his children. He would take out his Playboy books and show us pictures, and he would comment on the size and shape of people's sexual organs. He and my mother would also walk around the house naked in front of all of the children. Any time he was changing a diaper, he would play with the baby's penises. Often times, if he was helping you get dressed, he would "tickle" your vagina. He was completely obsessed with sex.

He would tell you stories about how in older generations, and other cultures, it was normal for a father to teach his daughters how to have sex. I was so young; I had no idea what he was even talking about at the time. All of his conversations revolved around sex, apparently to "groom" his children. He would repeat sexual stories he claimed he was told when he was in the Navy, or things he claimed to have read. He would collect talisman that were sexual, from China, and every conversation he had somehow had a sexual connotation to it.

Apparently, he had been cheating on my mother since the beginning of their marriage. She told me recently that she had found a book shortly after they had been married, and it included all the names and dates of women he had sex with while he was traveling. After he passed, it came to light that he kept that book, and added every event of abusing his own children! My brother also found multiple pocket books of unknown women when cleaning out the house years later. All of their identification and personal belongings were still in them. My oldest brother apparently has the book in his possession, it would be interesting to cross reference and see if any of them are on a missing person's registry!

When I was older, and he would start his conversation, trying to tell me about my sister Shirley's sex life, (he claims she would discuss it freely), I would let him know, that I will leave and not see him any further if he continued. I was not going to engage with any conservation with him in this manner.

There was a stretch of over ten years that I did not see my mother, not until I invited her to my wedding. We had been brainwashed into believing that my mother didn't want us, that she had abandoned us, and that she was crazy! Nothing could have been farther from the truth! She lived with a monster, who abused her and his children; he stole the ones that were still young, most likely so he didn't have to pay child support. My mother is also a medium, which made my father feel threatened. She wasn't crazy. But I do believe she has manic depression, as well as a hoarding disorder.

Both parents were very violent and abusive to all of us children. I believe my mother was violent and abusive because she just couldn't handle the chaos. I don't think she was as abusive with my older siblings, because things were still manageable, and my two younger brothers got away pretty much unscathed because they were young, and out of the house at five and six years old. I think my younger sister and I caught the brunt of my mother's wrath, and possibly my sister Millie. She used to beat us over the head with the heel of her shoe when she lost her temper. Sometimes it would be the hairbrush while she was doing our hair for school in the morning. I can remember going to the first day of school in my life, in my pajamas! I have no idea if it was a punishment, or she just didn't want to get me dressed. Other times, she would make us sit on the bathroom floor for hours as punishment and tell us to "wait until your father gets home!" My father would beat us with a leather strap used to sharpen a straight edge razor. It seemed that my brother Arthur and sister Millie got that the most. My sister would laugh at him when he would be beating her, and he would beat her more! It was like she was trying to prove that he couldn't destroy her. In the end however sadly he did destroy her and most of the rest of his children.

WHAT LIFE WAS LIKE AS A CHILD

A few times I can remember my parents getting dressed up in a tuxedo and evening gown, and going out to an event, most likely at the Masonic Lodge. My father had been a Mason since he was eighteen, and my mother was a member of the Eastern Star. My mother was already showing some mental issues back then. She was a clean person as far as her body was concerned, but she never took a shower or bath that I could ever remember. She believed that the water would irritate the moles on her body, and cause skin cancer, so she washed up with a facecloth. Back then she seemed to have thought it contributed to her brother's death. I hear different accounts about that. My dad seemed to think he died of black melanoma skin cancer, and that his body was completely black when he died. My mother, on the other hand, thinks he may have picked up a disease when he was in Korea. She also believes that her mother, my grandmother, contracted it from the body at the funeral home, and died shortly after. I believe she always regretted not going to her mother's funeral, but she said she was not going to leave the children home alone with my father and his mother. She was also pregnant at the time.

My father and youngest brother Albert were both past masters of the Masons. My father was master and secretary of several different lodges. He was also secretary of his last lodge, which entailed him being entrusted with many valuable antiques owned by the lodge. Sadly, my father disrespected them all! Not only did he live his life against all of their teachings, and principals, but my father was also a thief. I actually believe it was more of a compulsion like a kleptomaniac. He would walk out of restaurants with half the silverware, salt and pepper shakers, and anything else not nailed down on the table! It was like some warped game for him. My sister Shirley picked up his habit through life, and was arrested a few times for theft. He stole all of the printing equipment from the Masons, called an addressograph, as well as many other valuable items. When my youngest brother was cleaning out the house, he found multiple antiques and books that my father had stolen through the years from various lodges. He made sure they were all returned. My brother Albert followed in my father's footsteps, as did one of my sons, to join the Masons, and my youngest brother Albert proudly served as the longest past master for his local lodge. Fortunately he did not follow in my father's footsteps of disrespect, in fact just the opposite. My brother has made a point of living his life honorably, and he made sure everything my father had taken was returned. My father also had my nephew William Jr join the Masons at some point. This child became a career criminal with the encouragement of my father and his father (my brother William)!

As soon as we got up in the morning, if it wasn't a school day, raining or snowing, we were sent outside to play. We would scour the property for anything that was edible. There never seemed to be too much food in the house, other than the things we got from welfare, and with all those kids, it went fast! My father would bring home day old donuts, and I ate stale donuts and peanut butter until I couldn't stand either one anymore. The property, however, would have fruit trees from spring until fall. We would pick berries, apples, pears, plums, wild asparagus, and dandelion leaves to eat. We were expected to stay out until dark. On rainy days, my younger sister Shirley and I usually played in the house together, making blanket tents or playing with Barbie dolls. Millie was very in to knitting and crocheting, and it would keep her busy all day making clothing and afghans.

I'm not sure at what point my father started the addition on the new house on Maplewood Avenue, probably as soon as we all moved in. The house addition was an unfinished mess. It was a split level, and two bathrooms were just framed and plumbed. There was insulation batting in the ceiling, but no plaster board or lighting. The walls were the same, but had electrical outlets in them, with no covers. My mother's days consisted of loading us all into the car in the morning, and going to the city dump, to have us all help her pick through the garbage heaps! It must have been quite a sight for anyone driving in to actually dispose of trash! I remember how there were always hundreds of seagulls flying around our heads, and rats running out of the piles as we climbed them! There were big trucks all around us trying to push and bury piles of trash that had been there longer than the ones we were on. Years later, my father would insist my mother was having an affair with the man that ran the dump, ignoring her hoarding illness. She claims the man had no penis, because it was blown off in the war. Who knows, maybe they were both right!

We never went clothes shopping, except for shoes; everything else came from the dump. Both parents however, growing up in the depression and having shoes that didn't fit right, felt it was a priority for us to have properly fitting shoes. My mom did have a good eye for quality. A lot of the things she was bringing home became valuable antiques. Sadly, the moldy condition they ended up in, and the fact that the economy went the way it's been for so many years, and the fact that no one buys those things anymore, left them mostly with no value! The house was full, from floor to ceiling. In most of the rooms, there were piles and piles of stuff! We would walk onto a path of debris, to get from room to room and from one part of the house to another.

At one point, we had a cat deliver a litter of kittens. The mother got killed, and we could hear the babies crying, but we could never find them in the piles! Even the bed my parents slept in was loaded with stuff! There was just enough room to lie down. Clearly sheets were never changed after they were put on the bed. There was an exception to that however…

A TERRIFYING DAY

I remember when I was about four years old. My mother was about eight months pregnant. I guess she felt like she couldn’t take it anymore, constantly being pregnant, pumping out child after child, and not able to control the craziness happening in the house at the time with my father. She gave herself an abortion in her bed with a coat hanger. I can remember my older sister Gwen at the time, trying to keep me and my younger sister Shirley away from the bedroom, since we were hearing screams coming from everyone, and there was blood everywhere! We were both afraid of what was happening, and didn't know what to do! No one called an ambulance. One of my sisters called my father, who came home from work; it was about an hour ride. It was a baby boy. My father made a point of showing me and my sister, and then put the baby into the chest freezer in the basement. He said he was taking him to the doctor, to prove that my mother had done it on purpose. I don’t know if he did or didn’t. I do know the baby was in the freezer for a long time, right next to the Pepperidge Farm bread, and I do not know what eventually happened to the body. He apparently never took it to the doctor, because even my youngest brother remembers it being shown to him. When things like this happen when you're a child, you create a block in your mind. It's the only way to move forward, because you're too young to process what's happening. Years later, you learn to compartmentalize, because some things need to stay in a box in your mind! Knowing what I now do as a medium, I know my brother is safe on the other side.

My oldest sister Linda was not around much those years. My parents sent her to a private school, and she spent two summers in Europe. I remember watching the Mary Tyler Moore show, and thinking that she was basically my sister! They looked the same, had the same type of job, and I made believe that was her growing up! I remember my family always drove Mercedes, since it was part of their proud German heritage; they also let Linda drive one. I know she did get in a major accident when she was young, I think she was driving my father's car at the time. She was not in the house all that often since she was older and had her own life, and not home on this day. Apparently, she knew what was happening in the house, and got out as soon as she could.

DAILY LIFE

My younger sister Shirley and I were moved into the unfinished addition for our bedroom when the next two babies were born. We were less than a year apart by a few days, technically what they refer to as Irish twins. We only had one bed, a twin that we barely fit into together. We tried sleeping side-by-side and kept pushing each other out, and then we tried sleeping foot to head, and kept kicking each other in the head! I remember having a hard time sleeping at night, because it was right next to the kitchen. There were no walls, just framing, and a blanket hung. There also wasn't any heat on that side of the house at the time, and it could get really cold. My parents would sit at the kitchen table at night and go over the books for the business, and finances for the house. They were always fighting, I just don't remember about what. I remember my sister would wake up a lot at night, and claim she saw gray aliens peeking out from behind the couch in the other room. You could see the couch from the bedroom because the wall wasn't finished. I never saw them, but my mother tells me she did! Since I've met a Paladian guide, I guess I have to believe it now!

My older sister Linda moved to a finished room on the lowest of the split level as soon as it was finished. That area was finished a little bit more than where my sister and I were sleeping. It had paneling on the walls, and heat. My sister Shirley and I got bunk beds, and we were moved into the main house on the second floor, into Linda's old bedroom. My sister Gwen, and my sister Millie, both had bedrooms up there with us. We had a bathroom on the same floor for all of us to use, and we had a sink in our bedroom. We also had air-conditioning! I believe I was about seven years old at the time.

My older sisters Gwen and Millie both belonged to the Girl Scouts, and would iron their uniforms, and iron their hair at the same time! It was the thing to do back in those days. I believe my brother Arthur was also in the Boy Scouts at about that time. I remember that first summer was as close to "normal" as it ever got for me in that house. Millie, Shirley, and I would make creepy crawlers, and played with our Easy Bake Oven. I remember we also had a Ouija Board we tried to use as well. I remember the planchet flying around the board on its own, and we were all trying to figure out how it happened!

My sisters all played instruments for school as well, and they would practice every day after school. Linda played the flute, Gwen the clarinet, (which I played later on); Millie played the saxophone, and Arthur the trombone. Arthur never seemed to apply himself too much, and switched to the trumpet for a little while, and then quit all together. The downstairs area was finished a little bit better than the upstairs. Some of it was completely finished with walls and plaster. There was also another large living room with a fireplace, and a baby grand piano that my parents had bought years ago in their first house when they had no children. My mom tells me she used to love to play the piano, but I never heard her. Linda also took piano lessons as a child but the piano teacher refused to continue teaching her, because she said she scratched her piano on purpose with a key. We also had an old player piano in the basement that had the reel to reel. I just liked to sit and play the piano that way, because all I had to do was pump the pedals. I did teach myself to play a few songs on my own. I had the album of the musical Fiddler on the Roof, (one of my only birthday presents) and learned the songs by ear. Years later we had an organ when we moved, and even though I was only a child I would continue to teach myself the best I could.

THE DONUT SHOP

My father bought one of the first Mr. Donut franchises in the country in 1964, located in South Attleboro, Massachusetts. At the time, Route 1 was only a two-lane road, and 95 did not exist. He originally bought it with a partner with the last name of Kowalski. He formed a company called P& K Service Corp., after both of their last names. He claimed that his partner was stealing money, so he ended up buying him out. We'll never know if it was true or not, since my father was a pathological liar!

Other than learning how to run the business, my father had to learn how to bake donuts, which he did often when the baker didn't show. For the next twenty years or so, he always wore a baker's uniform, white shirt and white pants so the flour didn't show. I can remember him being so tired driving back and forth from the house on Maplewood Ave, which was about an hour drive, that he would jump up and down in the car seat while listening to classical music and whistling, so that he didn't fall asleep. I would never fall asleep because I thought he would crash the car, and I needed to try and keep him awake! Whenever we were home sick from school, we would have to go with my father for the day to the donut shop. I guess it was too much for my mother to deal with a sick child on top of all the rest of the kids. We would lie down on the flour sacks to sleep, in the storage room. I can remember one time, (he had bought a second donut shop in Woonsocket, Rhode Island), I was with him for the day. I was lying down, and got bored, or hungry, so I went to watch him make the donuts. I stood over the mixer, and my pink bubble gum fell out of my mouth into the donut dough! I wasn't going to say anything; I knew he would be pissed! Instead, as he started to roll out the dough, he hit pink gummy dough! I got discovered! He was really upset! If I wasn’t sick, I don’t know what he would have done! He had to throw it all out and start again. I remember another time, my sister Shirley got her hand caught in the car door, because it was parked on a slant, and we had to take her to the hospital to have it looked at. She got lucky and didn’t beak anything, but it swelled up like a baseball mitt!

The donut shops were open seven days a week twenty-four hours a day. My father worked seven days a week, all hours of the day and night, until the time he was too sick and too old to work. He took one vacation, and that was to a conference in Florida with my brother Arthur for a few days when I was ten years old. He had no sense of balance in life, and I don’t think he really cared.

All of us, even as children worked in the business growing up. All of us girls worked on the front counter as waitresses, most of us starting around the age of 15. I started a little earlier, at 10 years old.

When someone complained to the Board of Health that I was too young to be working with the public, my father put me in the bakery, to learn how to make the donuts. I wasn't strong enough at the time for the rolling pin, so I learned how to fry and finish them.

I can remember that many of the male customers were always trying to be inappropriate. They would try and grab you over the counter. Many of the workers were as well! One of his managers would make sexual innuendos and advances on me for over twenty years! Those were also the days that you were allowed to smoke indoors. I had a customer one time actually lay his lit cigarette on my hand while I delivered his coffee. I have no idea how it didn't end up all over him!

For the next two summers, I worked nights finishing donuts, and during the school year, I worked the counter on the weekends, starting at five o'clock in the morning. I was always an early bird and reliable. I got the shifts that no one else wanted. I found out that minimum wage was $1.95, when I was twelve. I told my father that I worked harder than anyone else there, and he was giving me fifty cents an hour, and I felt it wasn't fair. He agreed to pay me the minimum wage, but then informed me that I would be responsible to pay for all my own school clothes and supplies! He had no problem giving me tough love!

In later years, due to the location of the business, it would become the number one lottery dealer in the Massachusetts. It was pure luck and tenacity, because my father was really a horrible business person on so many levels. He was making close to a half a million dollars a year in profit, and never had any money! All the money he made, he funneled to my sister Shirley, my brother William, and his son William Jr.

The only other family member that was receiving a large sum of money was my brother Albert, who worked in the business as the general manager. He was admittedly overpaid, but at least he worked for his money. My father had been playing games with the business, and had put it into my brother's name without his knowledge. Clearly he did it to try and scam the government somehow with taxes. When my brother got divorced, it showed up that it was my brother's company, and my father refused to fill out paperwork for the courts to prove otherwise. My brother wasn't aware, only the lawyers knew. There-fore, his ex-wife was awarded a sum of money that was beyond what Albert made or could have paid. My father ended up paying it, but he denied that he had caused the problem to begin with.

I bought all my father's clothes for him from the time I was thirty, because he would always claim poverty, and walk around like a bum if I didn't. He would never spend anything on himself, other than dinner at a restaurant now and then. He was quite content to live in his dysfunctional world. I however, really didn't want my children to see him in that condition, while knowing I could have done something to help.

How the Donut Shop Affected Us

A few of us ended up with a good work ethic, almost to the point of being a workaholic ourselves, others, having had everything given to them, ended up being lazy alcoholics or drug addicts.
In later years, my father's financial help was solely dependent on how much you were sexually abused by him, or how guilty he felt about how you turned out. My sister Millie, who was diagnosed in later years with manic depression, was sent money to buy land and build a house in California. My youngest sister Shirley, who had multiple diagnoses, manic depression, schizophrenia, alcohol and drug issues, and paranoia, was basically funded with a house, multiple cars, jewelry, and whatever else she wanted. (I was her legal guardian for almost twenty years prior to her passing.) William was a dangerous alcoholic, who would threaten my father's life; thus again, given a house, cars, and funded into the hundreds of thousands of dollars to continue enabling his habits on a yearly basis. This led to him raising his son William Junior in the same manner, and funding them out of fear.
Linda and I survived, and seemed to have normal lives, despite our upbringing; hence, there would be no assistance for us! Arthur refused

to come around at all and asked for nothing like me. Gwen threatened to expose my father for the abuse, and tried, so she not only received nothing, he never paid her back the money he borrowed from her years earlier, and refused to speak to her until he died.

Apparently, Gwen had a shelf of toys fall on her head when she was about twenty years old, and in a Child World store with my brother Albert. When she got the settlement, my father said he needed the money, and borrowed it. He never paid her back. He also tried to deny borrowing the money! We only found out about it because when he was cleaning out the office Albert found a letter she had written him years ago, asking why he stole her money and treated her so poorly.

Sadly Gwen, the poor thing, has many problems, including alcoholism, and has lived off the system her entire life. She had child after child to stay on the welfare system. She ended up with three girls by three different fathers. When she needed money she prostituted herself. She used to take the kids into the bars and do the johns right in front of them! The children had been taken away on many occasions by Social Services, but they were always returned. When she couldn't have any more children, and they were all in school, instead of going to work, she paid someone to break her leg! Then she refused to go to the doctors to take off the cast, because she wouldn't be able to collect from welfare. The result of that was almost losing her leg! She ended up with a permanent deformity and on disability after all!

Arthur was a drug addict and thief when he was growing up. Around the age of nineteen, he moved out and got himself a job. He wasn't far away, but married a shrew of a woman, that dictated his every move. She forbade him to go visit his father, and she caused huge problems at my wedding. Arthur only started visiting his father briefly prior to him dying, and was stealing his clothes to sell on eBay! He very rarely ever stopped to visit or see how he was through the years. It was the same with our mother; he's only gone to visit her a few times in the nursing home. He still has issues with marijuana, but has managed to keep himself employed and out of trouble since his early adulthood. Sadly, however, he tried and failed at stealing our father's money along with my younger brother William and his son William Junior as our father was dying. Thieves are cutthroat, and they cut him out! Aren't some families lovely? I know at some point in time, their thieving lifestyle will catch up to them. Karma has her ways!

BEING KIDS

I remember whenever the weather was good, as soon as we get up in the morning and scavenged for something to eat, my mother would basically throw us out the door until it got dark. For the most part we didn't mind, we were kids. The house was built on a very large tract of land, I believe about six acres. It stretched from one city block to the other, and they had two rental houses that they bought on the other side of the block. Many times my mom would be at the rental property visiting with the tenant, and leave all of us kids alone in the house. The oldest one watching us at the time, my sister Millie, would have been about ten. In those days no one cared. Children were left home alone all the time.

I can remember one very stormy day, something happened in the house. I had to run across the field to try and get our mom from around the block. I was about five years old at the time. As I was running through the field, lightning struck right behind my feet, and sent me reeling through the air about ten feet. By the time I got to the house to get my mother I was a rattled, crying, shaken mess. I don't even think I could remember what the problem was at the house. Another time I felt something on my neck and ended up getting stung by a bumble bee. It’s still the only time I’ve ever been stung!

I don't remember seeing my brother Arthur outside very often with us. For the most part it was just us girls playing. I do however remember a time that my sister Millie and my brother Arthur were playing tag on roller-skates. The safe zone was the incinerator. Back then, it was legal for you to burn your trash outside. Apparently, my mother or father had lit the incinerator but hadn’t told anyone. My sister Millie came in on it going very fast and put both of her hands open face down on top. She burned them severely. I remember the pain she was in for months, and she wasn’t able to do anything for herself, because both of her hands were bandaged. She still had major scars when she was older. When I think of the pain that poor girl went through, for her entire life, her hands seem nothing more than a symbol of that pain. But through it all, she came out the other side an angel for others!

We had a lot of fruit trees and berry plants on the property. We couldn’t wait till they were ready to eat; it would be the only thing we would really eat for the day when we were outside. We would pick five gallon pails of apples, plums, and blueberries. One year it snowed in April, and killed the plum tree. We all mourned the loss, since for us, it meant a meal a day!

We did celebrate Christmas when I was very small, and would have a tree and a few toys, but no one ever had a birthday party or any other type of celebration. I was the exception to that however! I remember my older sisters planned a combined birthday party one year, for me and my younger sister Shirley. We were born four days shy of a year apart. They were running out of names by that time, and gave me the name June since I was born in June. She was also born in June the next year, and got the middle name May, because she was supposed to have been a May baby! Anyway, they really went all out for the party! My sister Millie baked a cake, with cooked fondant frosting! It was my favorite thing in the world! They tied strings all around the yard, and made us follow them to get our presents. I don't remember what my sister got, but mine was a ballerina pin with a broken foot, that had belonged to my sister Millie. It's still one of my most treasured possessions even today. I also got the *Fiddler on the Roof* album from my sisters Gwen and Linda. It was just us kids, no friends, no parents, no balloons, and no fanfare. They didn't have much to give us, but it was a very special gift of love to me from my sisters. Not something I witnessed very often. For the most part, we really lived in fear of the next beating, and scavenging for the next meal, honing our survival skills.

I remember my older sister Millie and I used to sit in front of the television in the morning, and eat cereal, holding the spoon between our toes instead of our hands! We all have long toes like fingers, and we thought it was hilarious! We never ate at the table in my house, since it was always covered in stuff! The food of the day was always either cereal, or day- old plain donuts with peanut butter. My parents were on welfare for quite a while, and I remember we would get white bread, powdered milk, and yellow cheese as well. Back then you waited in line at the distribution center once a week. It went quickly with eight children though! On the rare occasion that someone cooked something, (usually my sister Millie) she would stand and wash piles and piles of dishes for most of the day before she could. Otherwise they weren't washed for a week or more at a time. No one had chores to do, there was no order or cleanliness. My mother did do tons of laundry all the time though, and did her best to give us baths and keep our hair clean. No one from the outside knew what it was like, because no one was ever allowed in the house.

I was one of the lucky ones. I would spend as much of my time as possible at my friends' houses. They took me in, and showed me how real families keep house, how they interacted with one another, celebrated special events, and ate meals at a table. My favorite friend to visit and stay with as much as possible was Liane. Her family took me in like I was one of their own. They allowed me to stay at their house every day from the crack of dawn until dusk. They fed me, included me for Christmas, and holidays, and taught me how to eat with a knife and a fork at a table.

Liane's grandparents owned the local bowling alley and golf range. They had a deal with us on the weekends, when we got a little older, that if we picked up all the golf balls that got hit into the cemetery on a Saturday, we could bowl for free on Sundays. Her sister Linda was very good, and actually appeared on Candlepins for Cash! I don't remember if she won any cash, though. I can remember one Saturday we took her dog with us, and he started digging into a fresh grave. It got very overcast all the sudden and the wind picked, up, so we ran, and almost fell into another open grave! We told them we couldn't pick the balls up that day!

One day we were in her house playing in the basement, and her parents had gone out. (Again, kids were left alone all the time back then.) We heard someone in the bathroom, and then heard glass break! We ran outside, and saw a man peering out the bathroom window at us. We ran to her cousin's house around the block, and they called the police. They couldn't find anyone when they got there, and didn't find anything broken in the house. To this day, I don't know if it was a real person, or a ghost we saw, knowing that I could see them!

THE KIDNAPPING

When I was ten years old, my father packed the car with me, my older sister Millie, and my three younger siblings, and moved us all to a house he had bought between the bakery and donut shop in South Attleboro. My sister Gwen was already living in South Attleboro, but still in the basement apartment of the bakery next door. All we had were the clothes on our back. For years my father would tell us that my mother was crazy, and the she threw us out, because she didn't want us. You get brain washed into believing what you're told when you're that young, when you don't know anything differently. Since I never received any affection from my mother either, it was easy to believe. It wasn't until I started asking questions when my mother was ninety-two years old and in the nursing home, that I found out he took us because he was afraid of a divorce and child support. It makes more sense as an adult, since she would have at least packed clothes or toys for us! My sister Linda confirmed this as well when I asked her. My mother was at a loss as far as what to do at the time. I asked her years later why she let this happen to us, and why she didn't do anything about it to protect us. I almost felt bad for asking, as soon as it came out of my mouth. She broke down in tears, and said she had no job, and no way of supporting us. Our father would have ended up in jail, and she believed we all would have ended up separated in foster care. I'm sure she was right.

I can remember that when we would go to the donut shop with my dad before we moved, he apparently had a girlfriend on the side. I think her name was Joelle. She and her husband were living as tenants in the house at the time. I can remember him kissing her in front of me and my younger sister Shirley. I think Shirley was the one that told my mother. My mother was also starting to come into her own strength about that time, or trying to. My mom was not crazy, but she is a psychic medium like me. She started to go for training, which was very upsetting to my dad. She wasn't supposed to have a life outside of him. She told me he had cheated on her previously through the marriage; in fact he kept a log of it! At one point she found a book of his when he was working as a salesman, with notes, names and numbers. My father became paranoid that she was cheating on him, and started recording all of her phone conversations for the divorce. It seems a common theme, since my husband also accused me of cheating when he had been cheating on me! Since my father wasn't able to prove anything, he determined that she didn't want to be with him, and that she must be a lesbian, since all of her friends were women! His mind always revolved around sex, and only sex.

When we moved, I felt like I was being torn from my friends, especially Liane, since I felt she was more my family than my own family was. I remember crying so much, and asking my father to let me buy a parakeet of all things to give her as a goodbye gift! Of course as a child I had no idea how inappropriate that was! I made sure to get them a cage and all the things the bird would need. Her mother was so gracious to accept it and not let on that it was not something normal people did! I have no idea why I needed to give her a bird, it just felt like I didn't want them to forget me. Apparently it was a female, because they told me it laid an egg shortly after receiving it!

My father agreed to let me get a pair of mice. I used to walk around with the female on the back of my neck and play with her during the day. Apparently they were a male and female, because before long they had a litter of fifteen more! The mother killed the father, because he tried to eat the babies, and then she got out of the cage. My brother Arthur tried to catch her, and she bit him. My father was so angry; he said the mice had to go. We found out later what he did with them. He put them into the basement of the neighbor's house across the street from the old house in Holbrook, because he didn't like the guy!

Liane and I kept in touch for a while, but being kids, you lose track of each other. I remember sending her a wedding invitation when I married my first husband. As she came through the receiving line, I didn't recognize her. When she told me it was her, Liane, I just started crying and couldn't stop! I loved her so much growing up, she was my savior! I was just so happy to see her, and so honored that she traveled all that way and came to my wedding. I wanted to show her that I made it, I survived! We again tried to stay in touch, but she had her own demons to overcome. For many years however, whenever I was in the area, I would stop and say hello to her parents, and ask about her.

My sister Millie became our mother after we moved. She was fourteen years old at the time, very timid, and shy. She would cook breakfast for us, and dinner most nights, do our laundry, clean the house, and try to keep her sanity. It didn't work. Within the year, she ran away from home, to go live in the Hare Krishna temple in Boston. They then shuffled her to New York when my father started inquiring about having her return home, supposedly due to her age. It was a dangerous life for her; she was beaten, raped, deprived of food and sleep, and married off twice within the cult. This was all part of their deprogramming, or brain washing techniques. I didn't have much of a relationship with her for years for this reason. They justified stealing things all in the name of their god Krishna. When she would come back to the house for a night or two, under the premise of staying, or coming to visit Shirley, she always stole clothing or anything else of little or no monetary value that she wanted or needed.

Around that time my sister Gwen moved back into the house. She had been seeing a married man that was twice her age, named Andre Lafarierre, and had become pregnant. I believe she was seventeen at the time. My father offered to pay for the man's divorce if he married Gwen. He paid for his divorce, and the guy took off with Gwen, but didn't marry her. The next thing we knew, Gwen was in a mental institution somewhere down south, and Andre had put the baby in foster care. My father got Gwen transferred to a local private psychiatric hospital, and I got to raise my baby niece Lakshmana that summer. Gwen was also involved with the Hare Krishna, and this was an Indian name. They nicknamed her Lucky, which the boys made fun of when she got to be school age, so she later changed her name to Katie. Gwen was the person that got Millie involved with the Hare Krishna, and apparently they both got inducted through my oldest sister Linda, who did not stay in the cult. By the time September came, Gwen was back in the house and able to watch the baby, and I was back in school full time. I would make outfits in sewing class that they had back then, and I always made a matching outfit for my niece. I was always quite domesticated!

The Molestation

Since Gwen moved in with the baby, we were running out of bedrooms with everyone there. Arthur had also moved in, he had still been with my mother, but was thrown out of the private high school he was going to, Thayer Academy, for selling drugs. I ended up making a bedroom out of the living room. It had French doors on one side, and a regular door that connected it to the room Gwen and the baby were in. My father moved his bedroom to a room next to his office, in the space above the bakery. Technically there was no adult supervision in the house, except for Gwen. She had a boyfriend that would come and stay with her who was very abusive. If he didn’t like something Gwen did, he would beat her. All of us were concerned, and I would tell her it's not right and she shouldn't be getting hit.

My father always worked crazy hours, because the business was open twenty-four hours a day, seven days a week. A lot of times after I was up and off to school, he would go to sleep in my bed. I didn’t think anything of it. One morning, I was still in my bed, when he came in and lay down next to me. I was lying on my side, half asleep. Before I knew it, he had lifted up my night gown and pulled down my underwear. I was so scared I just lied there and pretended to be asleep.

He then asked me if I was asleep. I was frozen! I wasn't sure if I was dreaming. The next thing I felt was him forcing himself inside of me. Being that young, and being a virgin, obviously it hurt. I was so scared I just held my breath and couldn't believe what was happening! When he was done, he tried waking me up, to find out if I had started having my periods yet. I was like a zombie. I just laid there until he fell asleep, then I got up and got dressed to go to school. At the time I had not started my period yet, I was only ten, but my father made an appointment for me at the doctor. I felt like I was being violated all over again, going to a male doctor for an internal exam at ten years old. Come to find out, he had given me a case of the human papalova virus. I can't imagine what he told this doctor, who would have known after my exam that I lost my virginity! But no one ever asked me. It seems he gave all the girls the same virus, which eventually led to my sister Millie's cervical cancer and death.

I decided to move my bedroom to the attic. There was no chance he was going to go up there to sleep! Being young and naive, and being so traumatized by what happened, I was half in denial when I started seeing my father coming out of my younger sister's room in the morning. My older brother Arthur was not as naive however! I came downstairs to him making fun of Shirley coming out of her bedroom, after having sex with my father. He made some comment to her about him teaching her how to give a good blow job! She got really angry and started yelling at him. Like everyone else, I knew there was nothing I could really do, so I did nothing. I tried at one point to talk to Shirley, and she didn't want to talk about it. She was already not going to school. The truant officer had been to the house to see her, and she was hanging around with a girl that would later become her drug dealer throughout her life. I found a letter in her room talking about the drugs she was doing, which I told my father about. I know he asked her about it, because she went totally ballistic on me for reading her letter. The drugs, however, continued.

For many years I blamed myself for what happened. I'm sure many victims, if not all, do the same thing. I thought I should have done something differently. Maybe if I wasn't so scared, maybe if I hadn't frozen, maybe if I screamed! I had to forgive myself before I was strong enough to confront the monster! Confront him I did however. I was about twenty-five when I approached him one day. I wanted to know why he thought it was appropriate to violate and abuse his own children! He never apologized, instead mumbled something about thinking I was asleep and didn't know for all those years. I made it very clear that I did know, and if he ever tried to touch my brother Albert's daughters I would make sure he went to jail. His major concern was that I didn't tell Albert, because he didn't need to know. He wanted him to continue thinking he was someone he wasn't. I also made it clear that if it ever came up, and he denied it, I would let the world know! I took back my power!

MORE DYSFUNCTION IN THE HOME

Killing the Dog

Arthur was thrown out of high school for dealing drugs, and was heavily into using them around that time. He would sit out on the low roof outside his bedroom window with his friends, drink beer, and drop "window pane" acid. The only reason I knew what it was, is because he showed me how he put it into his eye. He would blast Jethro Tull on his stereo, scream, and act crazy. Many a night the neighbors would call the police and my father would talk them out of arresting him!

He had a beautiful German Shepard as a pet named King. At the same time, I had a Shitzu that I totally did not take care of. I was too young and should never have had a dog. She would stay tied up in the living room all the time, very rarely go out, and poop all over the newspapers. I had no idea how to train a dog, and I decided to take her to the dog pound with her papers, and give her up.

The German Shepard on the other hand was very well trained, and a wonderful watch dog. He lived under the front porch, and had an entrance near the basement stairs. One day a friend of my father's came by to say hello. He went over and knocked on the basement door, and King came out, doing his job, and bit him on the ankle. Not enough to break the skin, just enough to get his point across that he was watching the house. My father let my brother Arthur know, and told him he should be on a chain, or not able to get to the door. As I was watching from the window above, my brother grabbed a metal pipe, and proceeded to beat the dog to death in front of me! I was screaming, someone else in the house called the police, and he was arrested and charged with animal cruelty. I recently found out that my youngest brother Albert, who was only five years old at the time, watched it as well from outside, as did my father. Many years later, when I was trying to recover from my first husband's infidelities, I realized that I was also recovering from post traumatic stress disorder, (PTSD) from incidents such as this at home. As much as you try and block things like this, eventually you have to fully process and deal with them.

How Children Become Monsters

During this time, my youngest brother Albert was always with my dad, mostly because of his age, he was only five. My brother William however, being shy and withdrawn, became the target for a couple of very mean and vicious kids in the neighborhood. My brother Arthur would also get in on tormenting him for some reason. He would be locked in small spaces for hours, like under the porch, beaten up and bullied all the time. He never really learned how to fight back so much as he learned how to be a dangerous malicious person, with a lot of anger issues.

He started taking steroids when he was in high school and drinking. He was on the football team, and worked out in the gym every day. He stood over six feet tall, and had huge muscles. He became a very violent and dangerous person. He raped a girl that lived around the block when he was in high school, at a drinking party. He then started threatening her family. They knew my father had enough money to get him off of the rape charges if they pursued it, so instead they moved out of town.

When I was seventeen, he approached me from behind when I was cleaning my fish tanks. He had a French knife in his hand, and held it against my ribcage. He told me if I moved he would kill me. Then he told me I better watch my back, because he's the one in charge now! He was my number one reason for moving out of the house and in with the first guy that looked at me. I was afraid for my life. When I told my father what he did, it was the standard answer; "He didn't mean it, or he would have done it!"

This is how my father spent the next fifty years of his life, being threatened by my brother William and his son Billy Junior, my nephew. They would threaten to kill him, and he would say they didn't mean it! He would refuse to let me or my brother Albert intervene. My father always put more value on the boys in the family, because they carried on the family name. The girls had no value, according to him, other than to have sex and babies.

The Holidays

The first Christmas in the new house, we picked out a huge fresh Christmas tree, and my sister Millie helped us get it all set up in the living room. We had never had a fresh live tree before. We always had the silver tree with the color wheel when I was a kid. Albert was only five at the time, and still believed in Santa Clause. I went outside and made deer tracks in the snow, and then made it sound like there was a commotion around the Christmas tree. Millie put the Christmas presents out, and came down and saw the tracks in the snow, and totally believed that Santa had come!

It was an alright Christmas. We were pretty much intact, and the house was clean, Millie was playing mom, and my father got most of us presents. (I apparently didn't ask for anything). The following year however, everything had changed. He had already molested me, and I felt like the black sheep. He was molesting Shirley, although I was in denial about it, and she was using it to her advantage. She was staying out late and drinking most nights. On many occasions, he would open my bedroom door to see if I was in bed. I would go to bed every night at 10pm and get up for school at 6am. I would tell him to go check on Shirley, and of course she was still out!

She came home one night late, and he thought he'd use the old leather strap on her, that he used to use on the older kids when we lived on Maplewood Avenue. He couldn't find it, so he used his belt instead. Well, she spun around, and he caught her in the eye with the belt buckle. She had to go to the hospital to have it looked at. She made it very clear, that she gets what she wants, or she's going to tell what's going on, and he'll go to jail for child abuse! He was scared, and she was using it for all it was worth. The next Christmas, there were no presents under the tree for me again. But Shirley got a long black leather coat, a matching black leather pocket book, black leather boots, and Walki Talkie's! I remember I felt so unloved, that I actually pulled the muscles around my lungs crying so hard. Still, no one cared.

When I asked why I didn't get anything for Christmas, I was told it was because I still didn't ask! I never got a gift again. I knew that's not how it was supposed to work in a normal family. Funny though, I always got my father a gift for Christmas, until the year he died! Usually he got clothing, nuts, and chocolate. Just because he was dysfunctional, I didn't want my children to be raised the same way, and I tried to lead by example. He never really appreciated them however. In fact most years he wouldn't even open them in our presence. He would shake the box, try and guess what it was, and set it aside for later.

IT WAS MY TURN

Once Millie left, I became the next oldest, and the weight and responsibility of the three younger kids fell on me. I can remember standing there one day when the realization hit me at not quite eleven years old, that my childhood, such as it was, was over. I now had to be an adult. It was like something died in me.

I had no cooking skills, but someone needed to do the job. The first Thanksgiving meal I cooked was a disaster! Everyone brought their boyfriends, and Arthur brought his girlfriend. The tables were set up in the living room. The turkey was frozen, so I followed the directions, and thawed it in the bathtub. I stuffed it and made all the side dishes. Two hours after dinner started, it was still in the oven, and not cooked. We decided to eat all the side dishes and the dessert. Finally, the turkey was done. My father was all proud with his knife and fork and bragging about his carving skills that he had learned from his grandfather the butcher. When they got to the stuffing, there was a surprise inside! The bag of giblets! Who knew, I certainly didn't! So that summer, my father sent the younger three to summer camp, and I was sent to cooking school for the next three summers.

I did give it my best try prior to cooking school, though. A little after I got my first paycheck, I spotted a lobster in the window of the seafood store I used to walk past when going to a friend's house. I thought I could keep it as a pet! I had two thirty-seven gallon fish tanks in the house that used to belong to my brother Arthur before he moved out. I filled one with water, poured a can of Morton salt in, and watched the poor lobster turn blue right in front of my eyes! Oh wait! I knew you can also eat lobster if you can't keep them as pets! I put it on a cookie sheet and put it into the oven. When it turned red, I ate the claws and threw the rest away. I had no idea all the meat was in the tail!

I would do the grocery shopping with my father every week at Almacs, a grocery store in town. Back then you could buy store stamps and save them for china settings. I would collect all the stamps, and buy the place setting of china that they offered when you had the book full. I bought an old sea chest at a yard sale when I was thirteen, and that became my "hope" chest. My hope of a real life someday. It's the formal dinnerware I've used for the last thirty years with my children and grandchildren, Havilland from Germany. Like I said, I was always domesticated.

The next one to run away was Shirley. She stole money from the donut shop, and tried to claim it was me stealing it. I used to bring a metal can of Bigelo mint tea to work since I didn't really drink much coffee. She claimed I was stealing the money and taking it out in the can, and of course my father believed her. She took the money she stole, and bought a bus ticket to New York to see my sister Millie. She didn't find her right away, and sold her leather coat, boots, and pocket book for money to eat. She finally connected with Millie, who helped her get safely home. Shirley ruled my father however, and was going to do whatever she wanted. She didn't go to school after the age of twelve or thirteen, and instead she basically became my father's private prostitute. She was clearly giving him sex in exchange for anything she wanted, usually money for drugs and alcohol. This is the reason as that, as she got older; my father supported her to the tune of hundreds of thousands of dollars a year. He knew he caused her mental illness. I wouldn't be surprised if he was still sleeping with her up until the time his prostate cancer made it impossible, around the age of seventy-five.

MY FIRST BOYFRIEND

I met my first boyfriend Tony, when I was thirteen and working in the donut shop. He was eighteen and just graduating high school. He thought I was at least seventeen since I worked, and I looked much older. I wasn't going to tell him differently. We hung out in the parking lot with all of his friends on some weeknights and weekends. It was kind of like American Graffiti! They were all hard-working kids, who spent a lot of money on their cars. On the weekends they would race them on the highway. Tony had a 1957 Chevy that he would enter into the car shows, and he won a few awards for it. Since there was no supervision to speak of, I would go out with him on weekends, and we would make out in the back seat of his car. But he was always respectful when I said to stop.

About the same time, my sister Gwen got into a huge fight with my father. Apparently, she had been in a Child World store about a year earlier with my brother Albert, and some boxes had fallen on her head. She received a large settlement from the insurance company, and she made the mistake of letting my father borrow the money. Although my father was successful in his business, a lot of it was luck. He was a lousy business person and spent money like water. With him, it was always the best of the best, and price was no object. Gwen was not all that stable, even then. She had already been institutionalized a few times for mental disorders associated with drug use. My father was alienating Gwen, telling everyone she always wanted money from him. We didn't know she just wanted her own money back! My brother ran across a letter she had written him years ago, wanting to know why he treated her the way he did, when she was the one that had always been the victim.

She threatened to tell everyone what was going on, and took the first step that anyone had! I believe she called Social Services to investigate the home situation. I'm not sure exactly what she told them, but after asking us what was happening, and us all denying everything, they told him Shirley needed to be back in school, and there needed to be an adult in the home at all times. After finding out about the age difference between me and Tony, they required us to have a chaperone to go out. I ended up taking my little brother Albert everywhere with us for a few months. My father never spoke to Gwen again. He considered her just a trouble maker. I do not believe he ever paid her back the money he borrowed, either.

To rectify the situation, he moved a girl into the house by the name of Suzie. She was a large woman, and much younger than him. I'm not sure if she actually worked, because all I can remember is them having sex most of the time she was there. It didn't last long, but she did take me to buy my first bra. I probably should have been wearing one for a year prior, but I didn't really know how to go about it. I would just layer my clothes as much as possible. I got teased a lot in school, because I developed a little earlier than most of the other girls my age. I was grateful for the bra, and you know, everything happens for a reason!

When she left, he moved the next girlfriend in, her name was Nancy. She was again much younger than him, was divorced with no children, and hated kids. She would become his future wife, although I wouldn't find out he married her until years later. I believe he was still molesting my younger sister Shirley while these other women were in the house, just not as regularly.

The protocols put in place by Social Services didn't last long. Shirley was still bunking school and staying out nights, I spent two or three months with my baby brother going out on dates with me and Tony, and life went on! I was very fortunate that Tony was my soulmate. He was my world. He didn't stop seeing me when all this happened, because he genuinely loved me.

We were together for five years, and we saw each other every single day during that time, When the blizzard of 1978 hit, he walked about ten miles from his house in the snow to be with me. He came from a strict Portuguese family, didn't drink, smoke, or stay out late. He worked very hard every day at his mechanic job, and did auto bodywork on the side at night. I was always in bed by 10 p.m., and he always went home. We did go away on weekends with friends by the time I was about fifteen, but by then I was more like a twenty-five-year old!

Speaking of the Great Blizzard of '78, guess who was not home and in her bed! My younger sister Shirley wasn't! She was fourteen at the time, and someone found her passed out in the snowbank not far from the donut shop. They called my brother Arthur, who brought her back to the house. Her eyes kept rolling back in her head. I remember I was already asleep by the time they found her, and I got up from the commotion and then I went back to bed. I didn't stay up to see the ambulance take her to the hospital. She had a blood alcohol level so high she was lucky she hadn't frozen to death. They ended up pumping her stomach.

I remember we had a generator at the donut shop so that we could stay open, and my father was keeping the parking lot plowed so it was accessible. The police departments from Rhode Island and Massachusetts made it the drop-off point for emergency personnel, and were using snowmobiles to get people back and forth to the hospitals. They were also taking the nurses back and forth, and doing medication runs with the snowmobiles. We had plenty of hot coffee. We were also located right next to the highway. All the people that abandoned their cars found their way to the donut shop. I was cooking pot roasts at the house to feed everyone, since we had a gas stove. It was a crazy time!

One of our neighbors went missing at the height of the storm. When it finally died down, a search party went over with sticks poking the snow until they found his body, right outside his back door. He must have had a heart attack, and then froze to death. The snow was so high, that it went right over everyone's four-foot fencing like it wasn't even there. The drifts went from the rooftops to the street, and you couldn't see some houses. I hope to never see that much snow again! It was almost a week before the roads were clear and the cars were all towed off the highway! They brought in huge equipment from Buffalo, New York to move the snow. The equipment was so big going down the street that they had to lift the telephone wires for it to make a corner. The machines were so big, and there was so much snow, that cars were getting picked up with the snow and getting dumped into the Providence River. Most people had no electricity for almost a week. The only positive thing that came out of it was that people had to interact with each other, and take care of one another. That was a heartwarming thing to see.

Family life continued this way for a few years. We all learned how to do our own laundry. I would do the grocery shopping and cook, work at the donut shop on weekends, and see Tony every day. He would pick me up in the morning and drive me to school. We would sit and talk, then he would go to work, and I would go to school. The schools forbade him to park on school grounds, obviously, because they didn't like the age difference. Very bizarre, but we obliged and parked on the street. He would come pick me up when he got out of work, and we would go to his parents' house for dinner, and then either work on cars in his garage, or go to a friend's house and work on their cars. On Saturday nights we went out to dinner at Mon Kou for Chinese food, then we would go back to my house to watch television. On Sundays we would usually go for a motorcycle ride if it was good weather. In winter, we would go to a movie.

He was what saved me! He was my life, my world, my soulmate, my best friend, my mother, and my father all rolled into one! I was blessed that I met a man at that time who was faithful, honest, hardworking, and true. Unfortunately, as time passed, we grew apart, and he changed. It was not meant for us to grow together. We had separate journeys we needed to take.

I was working nights in the bakery, finishing donuts. I was sixteen. Tony had bought me a car to drive back and forth to high school, so I didn't have to take the bus. The timing was such that he was unable to drive me with a new job he had taken. We stopped spending mornings together. The baker I was working with at night was a man named Mark that I had known for many years. He had worked for my father years earlier, and then went into the Marine Corp. He was also older than me by about five years, the same age as Tony. When we were working side by side every night, we got to know each other very well and became close. He would call me on the phone on the nights he didn't work, and we would talk for hours, He was very sweet. Tony however, was not able to get through on the phone, and knew something must be up. We had a fight, and it just happened to be the weekend of a friend's birthday party. I went with Mark in his car, since the birthday girl was a mutual friend. Tony knew about the party and showed up there on his motorcycle. He was very hurt, and wanted to talk. I left the party with him on the motorcycle. In hindsight, it was a terrible thing to do to Mark, and he never really forgave me for it. It always caused that little something between us, that I would maybe leave him if we ever got together as a couple. But we didn't become a couple. We did keep in touch over the years, and through my first marriage on a fairly regular basis, until he married as well. Then more infrequently, until now it seems just at funerals. We'll always have a very special connection, however, on a soul level. He was truly a soulmate, just not someone who was supposed to stay in my life. He was a catalyst for the change that occurred.

Tony's family was very strict "greenhorn" Portuguese from the "Old Country" as they say. They never really liked me because I was not Portuguese. His father, a massive alcoholic, was always nice to me, as was his younger sister, but I could tell his mother only tolerated me. When it was time for him to marry, they put a lot of pressure on him to find a girl of the same culture. He had asked me to marry him, and bought me a flawless one carat diamond, for my sixteenth birthday. His family was going to Portugal for the summer that I turned seventeen. He told them he would not go unless I could come as well, and they refused. In fact, his mother picked up a chair and threw it at me after he asked! Things changed that summer, though I had a car and would go to his house and wait for him to get out of work. He would tell me that he was hanging on some street comer with his friends and would be there shortly. This was very out of character for him. Then one weekend, when I was working at the donut shop, in front of all our friends, he pulled up across the street with a girl on the back of the bike, wearing my helmet and my motorcycle jacket!

I felt like I had been stabbed through the heart. There was nothing to talk about with that kind of betrayal. I was a very black and white person, and there was no turning back. I sold the diamond ring within the next few days; back to the jeweler he bought it from. He found out, bought the ring back, and ended up giving it to the girl on the back of the motorcycle, Maria. Within the year, he married her in a large church ceremony. Later, she would come into the donut shop. I'm sure trying to get a look at me, and showed the ring to my sister, calling it "June's" engagement ring on her finger. How sad, not her own. The split was like a death for me. It took me one solid year to get over him and even consider dating anyone else. I was completely heart broken, but on some level I also knew it was for the best. We had definitely out grown each other. He allowed me to keep the car he had bought for me, which was a wonderful gesture on his part.

I would not run into him for a few years. I was at a company Christmas party when I was just about twenty, before I met my first husband, and had taken my sister Shirley with me. It was on open bar situation, and she was taking full advantage of it. There was a married salesman at the party without his wife; because she was due to have their first child any day. My sister Shirley went out to his car with him, according to what he told his co-workers, to give him a blow job. (I don't doubt it.) On her way back into the party, she cut through the restaurant. She came running in to tell me that she just saw Tony having dinner by himself in the dining room. Not having been able to get any closure from him, I immediately went out to see him. He told me he was there by himself, because his wife had just given birth to their first child, a son, but the child had died shortly after his birth due to a hole in his heart. My heart went out to him. I lived alone at the time, and he followed me to my apartment. The attraction was still there on both our parts, and we quickly ended up in bed together. It was like time hadn't passed. I wanted to know why it happened, how could he just find someone else and leave to marry someone else? I never really got much of an answer, other than the family pressure. He told me he never really wanted to marry her, but it took on a life of its own. He thought I would have showed up at the wedding in the last minute to rescue him, and let him know I wanted him back. Life doesn't always work that way.

Years later when I was getting divorced from my first husband, he tracked me down, after finding out. He started calling me on the phone every day to talk and see how I was doing. I finally agreed to go for lunch, and I asked what he wanted from me, as he was still married. He offered to put me up in a condo he owned in New Hampshire with my children, and find me a job, so I could be his mistress. I declined the offer. By that point in time, he had been doing drugs for a while, most likely cocaine. He didn't even remember being in my bed years earlier after his son died, because he was too strung out on drugs at the time. He stopped taking care of himself, his teeth were rotting out of his mouth, (although his wife was a dental hygienist), and there really was zero attraction for me anymore. We were not the people we were ten years earlier. We had a reunion of everyone that used to hang out at the donut shop about fifteen years ago, and although he's living in Florida, he came up to see everyone. It was nice to see him, everyone was surprised that we still talked and gave each other a hug. Apparently, he was having trouble with one of his children having special needs, so he had his hands full. I'll always be grateful for the time we had together, and I wish him the best in life. I learned what I needed to learn, and my journey continued.

LEAVING THE DONUT SHOP

Child Molesters as Teachers

After Tony and I split up, everyone in high school knew about it right away. I was a culinary art major, and the main instructor, Bill Carter, had known my father prior to me going to the school. My father used to sell him donuts for the restaurant Mr. Carter used to own. He was also the instructor for the cooking school my father sent me to during the summer for three or four years. He knew as well, that I didn't have a boyfriend anymore. Mr. Carter was my father's age, forty years older than me. It was towards the end of my junior year at high school, and I was exhibiting baked goods and cakes in a local cake show. Mr. Carter tried to corner me in the locker area and attempted to kiss me. I pushed him away! He was not very happy about it, and he started making comments about how he always had an eye on me, and how good we would be together. I didn't even know what to say, and left. For the next few days he would continue making comments and try to put his arm around me, whenever he got me away from the class. He then put a classmate's name on all the entries I had done for the show I was exhibiting at. Her name was Pam. When I saw the name change, Pam was standing in front of my exhibits, and Mr. Carter put his arm around her, looked me squarely in the eyes, and said "This could have been you"! I was hurt, angry, and afraid. I didn't know what to do.

There were a lot of illegal sexual acts going on in the culinary department. At least one, if not more, of the senior girls were having a sexual affair with one of the other married instructors. They would go in the office during class, lock the door and have sex! Even though there was contact paper on the glass doors and windows, you could still see what was happening. There was one other Instructor, who was not involved, who was in his sixties. He was a very quiet, fatherly guy that tried to ignore what was going on in front of his face. I explained that Mr. Carter had been trying to touch me, and kiss me, and was making advances, and asked him if he could help. His response was "There's nothing that I can do about it!" That was the final straw for me. I left school and did not return. I went down with my older brother Arthur that had been expelled from high school years earlier and took my GED. In fact, I had my GED long before the class graduated. I was able to look at a year book after graduation, and saw that Mr. Carter had every picture of me through the years in culinary and the graduation picture taken out of the book, like I never existed! He ended up divorcing his wife and marrying Pam as soon as she graduated. Now-a-day's, he would be in prison for child molestation, and statutory rape!

I attended every class reunion, and when the class committee didn't come through for the thirty-year reunion, I organized it! The committee I put together did a wonderful job, and we had the largest turnout yet, for a class of almost five hundred! I did have to chuckle a little, however, when one of them said she didn't want to invite or sell tickets to anyone that didn't graduate. I wonder what she would have said if I told her I didn't graduate either! But if not for me, there wouldn't have been a reunion! People really need to learn to think from their heart, not always from their head. I was inviting people that actually went to our junior high with us but not our high school! The whole purpose is to reconnect with people that you cared about during an important part of your life. It doesn't matter if they graduated, or ended up at another school. What mattered was the love we all shared that night. I even made some wonderful new friends that I didn't even know in high school! I'd say it was a win-win for everyone.

Giving my Notice

I gave my two-week's notice to my father for my counter girl position in his donut shop when I turned seventeen years old. I had applied for a job working for an ice-cream company, as their inside sales/office position. True to form, instead of wishing me well, my father told me I'd never make it, and I'd be back! Within a few weeks of taking the job, my younger brother William came up behind me in the living room while I was cleaning my fish tank. He had a chef's knife in his hand, and he put it to my side, and told me not to move. He then told me that I should be very afraid of him because he can kill me at any time, and he was in charge! He then shoved me to the ground and walked away! I was scared, he'd never been right in his mind! He was also lifting weights, and taking steroids, and was a pretty formidable sight for anyone!

I had been dating a guy that I had met in the donut shop for about two weeks, and as soon as this happened, I moved into his apartment with him. His name was Louie, and we had the same birthdate, but different years. This turned out to be a huge mistake and a major learning experience for me! I didn't really know this guy at all, and I didn't tell him that my brother had just threatened to kill me, and that was why I was moving in. He had a job and rented a small one-bedroom apartment from his uncle, who owned a large tenement building in Central Falls, Rhode Island.

As bad as my mother's house was growing up, I don't remember ever seeing cockroaches. They may have been there, but I didn't see them. This building was over run. No matter what you did, one tenant on the first floor kept breeding them. I was a clean freak after growing up in the conditions I did, so I would go crazy tearing things apart to try and eradicate them! He also chain-smoked cigarettes, which I couldn't stand. He had a lot of anxiety and nervous habits, and he was addicted to valium. We were only there a month when his mother decided to leave her abusive husband and move in with us. Being a small one-bedroom apartment the only room left for her to stay in was the living room, until she could get an apartment. That took her about two months. In the meantime, I realized where her son got some of his issues! She was a nervous wreck as well and also hooked on valium and cigarettes! Her husband that she was leaving was also physically and verbally abusive. His entire family apparently was a little nuts!

His uncle that owned the apartment building had married a prostitute when he was stationed in Italy during the time he was in the service. He brought her back to the United States, and tried to have a life with her. She was extremely possessive, insecure, and psychotic! They never had any children and were quite well-off financially. He had a small white poodle that he carried around and took everywhere with him. She was an alcoholic and also taking valium! She would call a cab and give them money to go to the liquor store and bring back booze. She would purposely throw herself down her basement stairs in a sexy negligee, that she wore all day and night, and then call her husband out of work after calling an ambulance. She was in and out of the mental hospital every few months. She would come by the apartment constantly when she was drunk, looking for her nephew to go buy her booze or get her drugs. Once she even slept on the floor outside of the apartment, because I refused to open the door. She showed up at ten o'clock at night in nothing but the sexy negligee! I didn't have a phone, because I couldn't afford one, and there weren't cell phones at that time. When Louie came home from work in the morning, he found her and took her home. Years later, when I was married and had children, I was in a department store shopping and I spotted her. I immediately had a panic attack, and was praying she hadn't seen me as I left the store.

Being the entrepreneur that I am, I decided to open a business in partnership with Louie. I had been working at the ice-cream company for a while, and I decided to open a sub shop. My father used to have a soft serve business called Dodo's in the building that housed the bakery for the donut shop and his offices. It wasn't being used or rented at the time. My father also had a bedroom on the second floor of the bakery building. He hadn't slept in the house with us kids in a few years. I made an arrangement with my father for a certain amount of rent, and was able to use the space with the equipment he still had.

I bought a used grill and the few other things that I needed. He still had the freezers and refrigeration equipment, and I was allowed to use that.

My father was helping me charge the whipped cream dispenser at one point, and the hose broke on the CO2 cylinder. Before it went through the wall like a rocket, it hit my foot. Since I didn't have a lot of time to get it looked at, I walked the best I could on it. After a week I finally went to the hospital, to discover I had broken it so badly that they would need to operate to reset the bones. I refused, and continued limping for another six weeks until I could walk on it. By the grace of God, it healed, and doesn't cause me any pain today.

The business went well, and we were able to move into a larger, much nicer apartment. That's when things went downhill quickly. Louie quit his job as soon as we moved, and said he was going to work full time in the sub shop. Prior to that, he was doing part time days and working nights, and I was working days at the ice-cream company and part-time nights at the sub shop. Then it came time to pay the rent for the apartment. I gave him the money, but he never paid the rent. The landlord came knocking on the door looking for it! He claimed the cable guy must have stolen it. Fast forward two weeks, I got enough together and gave him the rent money, and again, he didn't pay it. He claimed he must have dropped it, because he found a few of the bills blown against the fence near the Sub Shop.

He would show up at my work, and wait for me to go to the bathroom, and then go through my desk. At one point he found a bankbook I had, that I was trying to save money to get away from him with. He made me get the money out of the bank so he could buy a new television! The next day, he sold my car! He forged my signature, then sold it to a police officer that was having an affair with his sister. She had a two-year-old baby with him that she would never let out of his crib. She was also an alcoholic hooked on valium! I went to the police station to report it, and was basically told, "What do you want us to do about it? He's a cop."

Apparently, Louie also had a gambling problem, and had been playing cards every night losing all the money! I confronted him and told him I was leaving. He threatened to hit me, and a friend of his that was in the apartment at the time intervened. I left with the clothes on my back, and nothing else! I slept on my brother Arthur's couch against his girlfriend's (now wife) wishes for two weeks, and then was able to rent a furnished one-bedroom apartment. His wife didn't want me to stay any longer, because she didn't like me using hairspray in their apartment. If it wasn't one complaint with her it would have been another, she was just a miserable person. Louie's family was calling me at my brother's place, claiming Louie was in the hospital because of me, he had tried committing suicide, and I needed to come right away! I stopped taking the phone calls, and apparently he left town.

My Biggest Regret in Life

Louie ended up joining the service and left for boot camp. When he returned, he seemed at first like he had changed and maybe he had matured a little bit. Of course, I was the first person he tracked down! In a moment of weakness, and tired of being alone all the time, I ended up sleeping with him again, just once. In all honesty, being young and naive is not a good thing! We didn't use protection, and quite honestly, after what had happened to me with my father, I really didn't think I could get pregnant. I was wrong. I was eating Oodles of Noodles soup one night, as every young person has when they live on a limited income, and I broke out in a terrible rash all over my body! Who knows what they put in that stuff! I went to my Doctor's office the next day, and just by chance, they took a pregnancy test. It turned out positive. I'm not sure if it even registered in my brain at that moment. I was in shock. The last thing I was prepared for was to have a baby, unmarried, and have to listen to my father say what a failure I was again! I talked to Louie about "what if" I was pregnant, not telling him directly that I actually was. After having a conversation with him, I realized the last thing in the world I wanted was to have him back in my life again, in any capacity. He had a daughter all ready from another woman, and he apparently got a girl pregnant when he was in the service. Her father had owned a strip mall, and he thought it was his way to the family money. Instead she had an abortion, and said she never wanted to see him again. I realized at that moment, that my father's money was the lure for him wanting to be with me.

I decided to have an abortion. The only person in the world that I told was my girlfriend that gave me the ride to the Planned Parenthood Clinic the morning of the procedure. When the woman asked me questions for her questionnaire, she asked if I had ever been "raped". It was the first time anyone had ever asked. I must have hesitated when I answered, and my eyes probably started to fill up, because she looked up quickly, and although I said no, she knew it was a yes. She said she was sorry, and that they have counselors if I wanted one.

The procedure was horrible. I was only about six weeks along, but I knew I was committing a murder. I remember how much it hurt, and I actually screamed as it was being performed. The doctor doing the procedure started yelling at me to "shut up!" (Ironically it happened to be the same doctor that would later offer to buy my first child!) It's something I've carried with me my entire life, even more now that I see her on the other side. I didn't know then what I know now.

We always have free will. Mine took the only little girl I would ever have. Later when I had trouble getting pregnant in my marriage, I felt I was being punished for what I'd done. I'm sure I'm not the only person to feel that way. Knowing what I know now, I don't believe in abortion. However, if it was illegal, people would be doing it on kitchen tables again, and we would lose more mothers as well. Clearly it was part of my path, and she knew she wouldn't be staying here long. Children continue to grow on the other side, but by only about one-third of the rate they grow here. She would have been about thirty-six now, and I see her around the age of twelve.

Years later, my oldest son would ask my father for advice about getting his now wife pregnant. My father made up a story about my first boyfriend getting me pregnant and me having an abortion. My father never knew that I did, and it wasn't my first boyfriend. Even if my father had known, it was a horrible thing to tell my son, basically just to slander his mother! He never had anything good to say about any of his children behind their back. I explained to my son that he was probably getting confused in his old age and was remembering my sister Shirley. She had about nine abortions that I'm aware of, for her it was a form of birth control! At one point she actually wanted to get pregnant and wasn't able to. It was a blessing, since she wasn't mentally capable of taking care of herself, let alone a child. I never thought about it at the time, but it's quite possible that a few of those pregnancies could have been caused by our father!

Moving On!

All this and I was now only nineteen years old! I had no phone, no car, no clothes, but I still had my job at the ice cream company! I would ask people for rides, and walk when I had to, but I always got to work every day on time. I was now in my first apartment alone. Most everywhere I lived was haunted, but I didn't realize most places are, it was just that I could see or hear them. I came home from working some overtime at the ice-cream company on Easter Sunday, to find every burner on the electric stove turned onto high and the temperature in the apartment about ninety five-degrees! I certainly didn't turn them on, and no one else had access to my apartment!

A few weeks later, I heard all kinds of noise going on upstairs, and in the front hallway. It was late, so I didn't get up to see what was going on. It was a good thing I didn't! The apartment upstairs was being robbed! Who knows what would have happened had I opened the door, being a single woman alone. I moved into a bigger apartment in a better neighborhood the following month.

Right before I moved, my father, who had bought multiple cars for most of the kids in the family except me, offered to "sell" me a car he had taken back from my older sister Gwen. I took out a loan from the credit union, and bought the car. He later in life tried to deny that he charged me for the car, so I produced the loan documents for him. That was a common thread for him through the years. He would borrow large sums of money from me with no interest, but if I needed to borrow money from him, I had to repay him at the going interest rate!

It was a strange time for me. I was basically by myself, no boyfriend, living alone, and very lonely. I would go out with my friends and drink just about every weekend. Nightclubs and bars didn't "card" in those days. I can remember driving home drunk at night, and going down side streets at eighty miles an hour! If anyone had pulled out, we both would have been killed, it was extremely reckless on my part. My guardian angel was clearly watching over me! I can remember knowing at the time that I wasn't going to live to see thirty.

I remember coming home one night after going out from work, and not eating all night. I came home starving and half drunk! I stayed up just long enough to boil water and put macaroni into it. I fell asleep sitting up on the couch with the radio blasting and all the lights on. By the time I woke up, the entire apartment was full of smoke from the macaroni burning in the pan. I opened the door to the apartment and the outside door since I was on the first floor, and tried to let the smoke out. It was taking so long, I decided to just go to bed and pull the covers over my head! Well, I apparently let all the smoke up the stairs to the second floor, not out the door, and they called the fire department thinking the house was on fire! I was never so embarrassed in my whole life, when three gorgeous firefighters started banging on my door! I got out of bed, wearing a skimpy night gown, and opened the door, and had to explain what I did! They hauled in big fans to clear out the smoke, and then proceeded to bust me up, offering to go buy me a pizza! That was the last time I ever went out without eating!

* * *

The Next Business

That summer I decided to open an ice cream parlor where I had the sub shop previously with Louie. We obviously closed it as soon as we split up. I was talking back and forth with a salesman that I worked with, and he was considering going into the business with me as a partner. Our manager at the time also wanted to go into business with me, and he was telling the salesman that if he opened the business with me, the company would give him a choice, and he would have to leave. We doubted it was true, but he wasn't in a position to take a chance, since he had a wife, two children and a house to pay for! No sooner did he tell them he wouldn't go partners with me, the manager brought me into the office and said he wanted to open it with me. Never being someone to mince words, and knowing that he was a raging alcoholic, I told him in no uncertain terms, that it would never happen! He wasn't very happy. As an employee, we were allowed to take one gallon of ice cream a month as part of our benefit package. We could take it as two half gallons, four pints, or one gallon of eight cut slices. I took mine as eight cut slices, and had it delivered at the same time as my ice cream order to the business. The Manager was aware that I had done this, and it was within company policy. After declining his offer to go into business, he abruptly fired me, claiming I stole it!

Needless to say, it didn't hold up at the unemployment hearing! I also called the owners of the company, and informed them about what had happened. I had been the top inside sales rep for the entire company, for the last two years. I was the sole person responsible as to whether or not the other employees of the branch received monthly bonuses. I had also won a fully paid trip to Disney World, for being the top salesperson in the company. They didn't want to hear it. It took about six months, but that branch fell apart. The manager had been stealing and doing drugs, and the owners were calling me to apologize and see if I would take my job back. But by then I had moved on to bigger and better things.

THE CONVERSATION

I was nineteen I won the free trip to Disney World. It was all expenses paid for two people. I brought my sister Linda with me. It was the first time we really spent any alone time together, and she asked me if Dad had "touched" me. I told her what happened, and she then proceeded to tell me that he had also molested our sisters. She told me at one point she walked into the bedroom and found my father on top of our sister Millie. She pulled him off and threatened to tell everybody! She was then torn whether or not to inform the authorities, and have us all put in foster care, or do nothing. She said she discussed with her husband the chances of them adopting us, and he made it clear they were in no position to take on that responsibility on. She chose to save herself, which was the best thing she could do at the time. As soon as she graduated high school, she met a man that she married right away. It's funny the things you do to escape and survive. Fortunately for her, even though they've had struggles, it's worked out. I almost wonder if it was out of spite for my father, since he told her it was a big mistake and it would never last! He was always so full of encouraging thoughts!

I can remember her coming back to the house one day with her future husband, and they arrived just in time. (She had moved out of the house into a basement apartment at the bakery.) My mother had my sister Gwen by the throat, and she was strangling her and pushing her backwards, and over the railing on the second floor balcony. I remember someone called the police, I don't remember who. Apparently my mother knew that my father was molesting Gwen, and believe it or not felt jealous! I think her mind had snapped at that point, from the stress she was under. Not being able to protect her children, not being enough for the man she married, and not being able to get away from the monster that he was. I didn't understand everything that was happening at the time, but my memory of it is very clear and years later all the pieces fit. My sister Gwen left the house that night, and went to live in the basement of the bakery as well.

My sister Gwen was extremely talented. We all seem to be if we apply ourselves. She would make the most beautiful drawings and paintings, she was very creative! One Easter, she decorated Easter eggs for all of us. We each got out own individual egg, that she comically put together. The only one I really remember was mine. She had taken a little bit of a cutting from the inside of my sister Linda's fur coat that she had, and glued it to the egg as a shawl. She named the egg the "Rich Bitch!" It seems laughable now, but I had a lot of jealous people calling me that when I was working my tail off in my businesses! If I had been a man, they would have said nothing, but because I was a successful woman, it was a different story.

Gwen was always a "poor thing" growing up, though. She wasn't a strong person, and what my father was doing to her showed all over her face. Every school picture she has showed the dark circles under her eyes, from him abusing her all night, and her never getting any sleep. She had trouble concentrating in school, and would occasionally get into trouble. I remember one day, she never came home from school. My mother called the police, and they found her in the closet in the school crying, at about ten o'clock at night. The teacher had put her in there to punish her, and forgot she was there! I'm sure it was very traumatizing to a twelve-year-old girl. Now a days the teacher would be reprimanded, but back then they could hit you and get away with it. It was considered acceptable.

I don't have much of a relationship with her, and I haven't since I was about twelve. She would have been about nineteen at the time, and I found out she stole my identity for a credit card. Apparently her credit was already destroyed at that age. She spent many years in and out of abusive relationships, having sex for money, and being put into mental hospitals. She always had such low self-esteem, that she let men take advantage of her, and she did it right back to them.

She had three children with three different fathers, one of which is still in question. At one point in time, she married the father of her youngest daughter when she was pregnant. He was in the military, and Gwen and the girls moved to Germany to live on the base with him. Apparently she was causing a problem with the wives on the base, servicing their husbands during the day! She was thrown off the base, and sent back to the United States. Her husband subsequently filed for divorce. Fortunately for my niece, he took custody of her at around the age of ten, and she had a half way decent upbringing. Unfortunately, she also ended up with manic depression, and although she had a pretty good military career in the Air Force, following in her father's footsteps, she ended up with a disability discharge. Gwen functions from day to day as best she can, but is on a lot of medication, and extremely high strung. Her reality of life is not always accurate. She visits our mom in the nursing home once a week, and calls her every day, so she has someone to listen to her daily tale of woe!

MEETING MY FIRST HUSBAND

Before the unemployment claim went through from being fired, I needed to work and have income to pay my bills. I would never ask for money from my father, or anyone else, I was very stubborn, and had difficulty feeling like I deserved help. For some reason I felt I would "owe" someone forever if I took anything from anyone. I asked my father if he needed help in the donut shop, which he always did, and I was able to work a couple of shifts overnight, that no one ever wanted to work. I also took a job that my younger sister Shirley got for me, at a Chinese restaurant where she worked. I was there about a week, when a guy came in for dinner with someone I thought was his mother. I mentioned to my sister that I thought he was cute and, was going to give him my phone number. She informed me, since I was a little naïve, that the woman was his girlfriend, not his mother, and they came in every week! I later found out that the girlfriend was actually older than his mother. The next night, he came into the donut shop when I was working. He was a truck driver from the area, and stopped in to have coffee with his coworkers. He recognized me immediately from the restaurant, and asked me out for dinner on the following Saturday night. I figured my sister must be wrong, and said yes. We went out and had an absolute blast! He was a complete gentleman. He had traveled extensively and was a great storyteller! He seemed very worldly to me at the time. We had a little talk towards the end of the night, and I told him that my sister thought it was his girlfriend with him in the restaurant. He admitted that it was, and that they had been living together for five years. I told him that I would not see him again if he was in a relationship. He said he had been thinking about moving out, and if that's what it would take to see me again, that's what he would do. Of course, I had my doubts, but that weekend he rented an apartment and moved out! But he never spent a night in it, he stayed every night at my apartment from then on.

I believe we met around mid-November, not too long after his birthday. By January he asked me to marry him, and I said yes. He bought me a beautiful one and a half karat diamond engagement ring. We had set the wedding date for a year and a half out, but by March he wanted to move the date and get married as soon as possible. (It never occurred to me that he was always drunk when he discussed getting married). He got rid of the apartment he never slept in, and moved in with me. It was a small but quaint one-bedroom apartment, above a shoe store.

When we were going through marriage counseling with the church prior to the wedding, the minister gave us a book to read. I took it home, and put it on the kitchen table. It was never to be seen again! I'm not sure where it went, we never found it, and had to explain it to the minister! Every now and then something of value mysteriously vanishes in my life, never to return! I'm not sure what prankster spirit is responsible, but it would be nice if it stopped!

We got married on September 15 of that year. I had known him less than a year, but I knew I was supposed to marry him. I was happy, I was in love, for the first time in my life. It was like I was walking on air! I knew he was my soulmate, and that we were supposed to be together. Throughout my life, I've always just known certain things, and this was one of them.

We were supposed to go to Hawaii on our honeymoon, and already had a deposit on it. Both of us had always wanted to go. We were paying for the wedding ourselves, and it was costing us about ten thousand dollars. That was a lot of money back in 1984. I thought it would be kind of foolish to spend all that money on a honeymoon in Hawaii, and then have to live in a small apartment when we came back, so we decided to buy a house instead. We didn't know if we were even going to take a honeymoon, it all depended on how much money was in the envelopes after the wedding! As it turned out, we had enough to take a nice drive down to Florida, and spend a week exploring!

The First House

When we got back from the honeymoon, we moved into the first house I ever owned It cost $50,700. Now lots of cars cost more than that! I needed a job to be able for us to qualify for the mortgage, and I had been out on unemployment for some time. The only place that would hire me right away was a car dealership. I knew nothing about the car business, but I sold a car the first day I worked! They were so thrilled, they gave me the keys to a brand new Charger and told me to take it for a ride. I learned how to drive a standard a long time ago, but I was never very good at it. I took the car out to the main interstate, Route. 44, because that was where the dealership was located. I think I was doing fifty and I was only in second gear! The speedometer on the car went up to 180! I turned around and came back, feeling very anxious and nervous. When I got to the red light, I had a big tractor trailer truck behind me, and I was very nervous about feathering the gas and the clutch. By the time I pulled back into the dealership, I was as white as a sheet! I handed them the keys, and decided it wasn't the job for me! We got the mortgage through the bank already however, so

I was able to leave.

During the mortgage process however, we had a run in with the bank and the mortgage underwriter. It seems like nothing can ever go smoothly! We were dealing with Old Stone Bank at the time; they've since gone out of business. The woman that was handling the loan kept asking for more and more documentation. Most of what she asked for was standard, such as tax returns and paycheck stubs. Then she started asking for letters from our employers to prove we actually worked at the companies that the W-2's were from. Finally, I asked her point blank, do you think we somehow forged our W-2 forms? Her answer shocked me! She said "Absolutely, I find it hard to believe that an uneducated truck driver makes more money than I do!" That was the final straw with dealing with that bank. I wrote a letter of complaint to the banking commission, was refunded our mortgage application fee, and got a loan through a credit union. Some people are amazing.

Funny Things that Happened During the Marriage

It was wonderful to have our own home. He loved working in the yard, and we enjoyed having a place to have parties and entertain our friends. I remember shortly after moving in, with us both working, I really only had time to grocery shop once a week. After growing up without much to eat, I found that I would hoard canned goods and non-perishable items in the basement. I would have cases of different things, so much that my sister Linda would fill a bag for herself when she would come and visit. I got home a little late from work one day, and didn't know what to make for dinner, since I hadn't had time to grocery shop that week. I decided to make waffles for dinner. After I had them made, I had second thoughts. I married a truck driver; surely waffles weren't going to be enough for him to eat! Under a panic, being a new wife, I went through the canned goods to see what else we had that I could serve with the waffles. The only thing I could find was chili! This combination became a running joke with him and the kids for years!

The other blunder I pulled as a new wife, was trying to clean his pillow. It was his prized possession, made by his grandmother. Supposedly she raised the chickens to pluck the feathers to make him this pillow when he was a child. She had long since passed on to the other side. I put the pillow in the brand-new washing machine, and washed it on a gentle cycle. I remember I had to do it twice because the water was black the first time. It didn't spin really well, because it was so heavy, so I let it sit and drain for a while, before throwing it into the brand-new clothes dryer. I started it up, and went upstairs to take care of something else. I remember walking outside for something, when I saw a pile of sawdust on the ground about a foot high right below the dryer vent. I ran inside to check the pillow in the dryer, but there was nothing more than a load of sawdust and feathers filling up the lint trap and every inch of the dryer! There was no way of cleaning it all out! Now I had to figure out how to tell him what happened to his pillow! He was so angry with me he wouldn't talk to me for almost a week. I truly thought he was going to want a divorce over it! He couldn't care less about the fact that I broke the dryer and needed a new one; all he wanted to do was grieve his pillow! Ahh, true love!

There was also a little episode that had me thinking again about life and death. My husband and I enjoyed motorcycle riding. I had always been on them with my first boyfriend, and we had a lot of mutual friends that were involved with them. We had a friend that owned a motorcycle shop in the Olneyville section of Providence, Rhode Island. It wasn't a very nice area, even the high school across the street had a metal detector thirty years ago! I had been sitting in the shop behind the counter, waiting for the guys while they went into the back room for something. Someone started to come into the building, and briefly opened the front door, and then ran off. Minutes later, the police came into the building. They stated that there had been a drive by shooting, and they were looking for the gunshot that came into the building. They found it! When the man opened the door, someone had fired a gun, and the bullet was lodged in the back wall, about an inch over my head! The scariest part is that I didn't know. It was the last time I ever went in that area of the city again.

MY BACK INJURY

I decided to work through a temporary work agency that places people from temporary to permanent positions, after we moved into our first house. They placed me at a company called Swarovski America. At the time, they were the largest jewelry manufacturer in the state of Rhode Island. I started out in the accounts receivable department, making phone calls for collections, and stuffing envelopes with statements. I was so efficient, that I was done with my work in half the time they expected, and was always looking for something else to do. Apparently, the human resource manager noticed, and asked me if I'd like to train for a payroll clerks position they had available. It was a permanent position, so I received a nice pay raise and benefits. I was twenty-one-years old at the time, and I loved working there, even though the workload was immense. I was eventually promoted to the payroll supervisor, and I was running the weekly payroll for the factory of about 800 people, the bi-weekly salaried employees, and the commissioned sales people across the country. I had no help and no back up, other than my boss who trained me. His name was Jack, he was about 5'1", and had weighed about four hundred pounds before having a gastric bypass operation. He had a bad toupee, curly grey like a clown wig, and a tick that every time he talked to you he pointed his index finger at you, and made a weird noise while he spit on you! His suits were also hanging off his body, because he wouldn't buy new ones after losing the weight. He was going through a divorce, and was constantly broke.

The office I had was very small with no ventilation. Back then the computers were large main frames that stood floor to ceiling, and the printer was the size of a couch! I used to keep my door open just to have air circulating when everything was running. At some point, I turned my body to get a paper off of the printer, and I had about fifty pounds of payroll registers in my lap. The chair wheels caught on an old rug on the floor, and the chair flipped. I knew I was hurt, but I didn't know how badly. I went into the human resource department to report it to the girl in the office and my manager. Jack came out and started laughing at me, asking what I thought I was going to do, since I had no back up! Being a little young and naive, I went back to work.

I've always been the one to "buck it up", and not complain. My father always said not to let your employer even see you take an aspirin. I also have a very high threshold for pain. That said; my back was really hurting! I ended up going to a chiropractor the next day. A few weeks later, they fired Jack, and replaced him with a woman that was friendly with the treasurer. She had no background for the job, and knew nothing about the payroll department. For some reason she felt threatened by me, and the fact that I had much more knowledge than she did. I felt it right away.

During all of this, my husband and I were trying to have a child. I was having difficulty getting pregnant, and we were both going through infertility treatments. They usually treat both people at the same time, that way they don't waste time determining where the problem is. I really felt that I wasn't getting pregnant as a punishment from God. My husband at the time had a very low sperm count, and needed to have variceal surgery. At the same time, I was having a dye test done to see if there were any blockages in my fallopian tubes. His surgery went fine, but my test was a different story. I was told it was a minor test, I could drive myself there and back. But after the test I was so sick and weak that I couldn't get off the table for over an hour! I was in no condition to drive. I ended up having to call my sister Linda, who worked nearby, to take me home, and get my car the next day. The nurse informed me that I may be allergic to the dye, because that wasn't a normal reaction.

Back at work, my new boss lady, offered to get me an assistant to help me out in the payroll department. Being psychic, I knew she had a motive. She wanted me to train the girl as my replacement, so she could fire me! I knew it as soon as the girl started working. I had no input as to who was going to be working with me, and the girl was not very competent. She was one of these people that think they know it all, so they don't have to pay attention. Needless to say, after four weeks of training, she went back and told the boss lady that she knew the whole job good enough to let me go! I was taken into her office, and told I can give my two weeks' notice or she would fire me. I asked on what grounds, since I do my job very well, and never miss work. I was then told that she didn't need any reason, and that I was one of those spoiled people born with a silver spoon, and that things just fall into my lap! She told me that I'm just good at everything I do, and I can go find another job, because everyone just gives me everything! The bottom line was she was jealous! I couldn't believe it! I told her I'd give her the two weeks' notice, and went back into my office stunned! I've had to work tooth and nail for everything in my life! Then I thought about what happened, and got really angry! How dare she treat me like that, she doesn't know me at all! I took all the notes I had on the job, all the lists I had compiled, and shredded them all! Let them do it themselves! After she went upstairs and told the treasurer what she had done, (he must have informed her that it's a dangerous mistake), she came back and said that she would pay me for the two weeks and I could consider it my last day. The next week I got a call from the computer room manager. He was always friendly and helpful to me. He was just checking to see how I was, and letting me know that the payroll department was a disaster; no one was getting paid for another week! He said the assistant didn't know what she was doing, and they had to hire an outside company to do the job. They also fired the assistant they wanted to use as my replacement! I heard the boss lady didn't last too much longer after that, either.

It worked out well. I immediately got another job through the same temporary agency as an office manager for a fabric importer out of Italy. Just as I took the job however, I found out I was pregnant! Swarovski also stopped paying the chiropractor bills for my injury as soon as I left. The chiropractor wasn't really helping much, but now we couldn't do an x-ray because I was pregnant. I continued to see the chiropractor through the pregnancy, but was in such pain that I was confined to bed rest the last two months of the pregnancy.

I also had to file a workers comp claim in court, due to them not covering the medical bills. The courts move very slowly no matter what state you live in! As soon as the baby was born, and I was able to go for testing, it was determined that I actually had a ruptured disc in my back, and two others that were bulging from the injury. Of course then there are the crooked insurance doctors they send you to trying to claim there's nothing wrong because you can walk , talk, and chew gum! They don't feel that they should have to look at the fact that the x-rays show an injury!

By the time I got to court, the baby was born. We named him Robbie. He was an absolute miracle! When I first got pregnant, I had a male OB-GYN, by the name of Lowe. I started bleeding, so he sent me for an ultrasound of the baby. Apparently, because I did the dye test, it caused multiple eggs to release into my uterus. I didn't have one baby,

I had four babies! One was what was called a blighted ovum, which means it didn't really implant fully. That left me carrying triplets. I thought I was hearing wrong! I was bleeding because one of the triplets was miscarrying. That still left me with twins! Of course I was so excited, I was asking my parents if they ran in the family, and couldn't wait. Fast forward a couple more months, and I started bleeding again. This was a little different; it looked like there was mica in the blood. I think it must have been around the five-month mark. I went for another ultrasound, and to see the doctor. He informed me that I was slowly miscarrying one of the twins. I was in shock! I didn't even know what to say. I left and went to a dentist appointment for a cleaning. I was there for a few minutes in the chair, and then just lost it! I started crying, and telling the dental hygienist what had just happened. Cell phones weren't common then, so they offered to call the doctor from the dentist's office. I called the doctor's office, and they got the doctor the phone. I asked if I was going to lose the other baby as well. He said he had no idea. He said the condition is so rare, that all we can do is wait and see what happens. I went from being so happy to be pregnant, to not knowing if I was even going to keep one. Then there was the back issue that was causing me so much pain on top of this worry. It was a difficult time.

When Robbie was finally born, I refused to let him leave my side. I kept him in my room, and if they needed to bathe him or weigh him, I told the nurses I would bring him down to them. My husband was joking saying I was acting like someone was going to steal him! It was just a feeling I had. Apparently, my psychic intuition was kicking in. I only stayed in the hospital for one day; I couldn't wait to go home. He was born on December 18, 1986, and we went home on December 19. On December 20, a baby was stolen from the Woman and Infants Hospital. A woman dressed as a nurse, went into the room and took the baby from the mother to give him a bath. It was a week before the baby was recovered. One of my lessons in life, as is everyone's lesson, is to listen to your intuition! That is your psychic ability!

When I went for my six-week post-partum checkup, the doctor, Lowe (who was not the one that ended up delivering the baby) asked me if I wanted to sell him for ten thousand dollars! He said he had plenty of people looking to buy babies. I was stunned; I didn't even know what to say. If I had been a little older, and a little wiser, I would have called and reported him to the licensing board. It didn't take much longer for him to be disbarred, however. According to the newspaper at the time, he had a cocaine addiction!

ROBBIE'S SURGERY

Robbie was not a completely healthy baby. I tried nursing him right after he was born. He would nurse constantly, and then projectile vomit the entire feeding across the room! It was all I could do to keep up feeding him. He was a week old on New Year's Eve 1985. I called the pediatrician's number, and was told to take him to the emergency room if I was concerned. That seemed to be the case every time I called this pediatrician. He wasn't our first choice he was a politician part-time, and it seemed to cut into his practice. Our first choice was a pediatrician by the name of Dr. Utter. He was getting on in years, and I was afraid he might retire before my children grew up. (It ended up that my three boys were his last appointment on his last day before he retired, some sixteen years later.) At the three-week visit for the baby, I explained the vomiting, and that he would scream uncontrollably like he was in pain afterwards. He assumed it was gas, and told me to give him Mylacon drops. He also noticed he had a tied tongue, as do I, and wanted to cut it right there in the office! I absolutely refused, knowing how many blood vessels are located under the tongue, and how dangerous that could have been! I decided to change doctors, and go back to my first choice, Dr. Utter. Thank goodness he still was able to take us as patients. The next Sunday, Robbie went into a screaming painful fit that wouldn't stop. I called the doctor's office, and immediately was told to bring him in! Mind you this was a Sunday, I wasn't told to bring him to the emergency room, but to the office, and the doctor would meet me there. It was an associate of Dr. Utter, a very nice and knowledgeable woman. She found that Robbie had a double strangulated ingrenal hernia! She called the hospital to make all the arrangements, and Robbie was taken to Rhode Island Hospital. Hasbro Children's Hospital didn't exist at the time.

As soon as we got him there, I left him with my husband, and went home to get clothes to stay the night. It took about forty-five minutes and I was back. I walked in and didn't see Robbie. I asked where he was, and my husband said they took him as soon as I left, and pointed to a room down the hall. I went over and peered in the window, and saw Robbie tied down on a stainless-steel table. I walked in, and saw one nurse holding him down screaming, and another nurse trying to stick a needle in his leg. His head had been shaved on one side, (he had been born with a full head of long black hair) and I asked what the problem was. Could they not find a vain? I was told that wasn't the problem. They weren't able to hold him still enough to get the needle in for the IV. I asked to see the doctor in charge. I was like a lioness protecting her cub! This little tiny Jewish man with a beard and a hat came over to see me. I asked if he was the doctor in charge, and he informed me that he was the senior resident. Not knowing what that meant at the time, I asked him if he was a full-fledged doctor! He assured me that he was, and asked what the problem was. I explained that they had already stuck my son seven times trying to get a needle into him for an IV, and apparently, they can't hold him still. (I wasn't aware of this at the time, but they're supposed to stop after three tries with the needle.) He offered to do it himself. I told him that I would hold Robbie, and he has one chance to do it. If not, they can wait until the anesthesiologist comes in for the surgery the next day. I held him, he put the needle in, and I handed him off to the nurse next to me. I then turned around, walked out the door, and passed out cold on the floor! I was working off of sheer adrenaline to protect my son, and it was too much for me!

His surgery was a success, and he went home in a few days. He was in what they called the Old Potter Building at the time, and the heat was over a hundred degrees in the dead of winter. They couldn't regulate it so they had the windows open. There wasn't much space in his room, so the nurse kept telling me I had to leave and couldn't sleep in the chair in the room. The nurses had Robbie literally pinned down in the crib so he couldn't move. I ignored them all, unpinned him, and slept with him in my arms. I got used to that; he slept that way for many months! None of my children slept through the night until after a year old. Robbie also had severe allergies, so he had his tonsils and adenoids out at twenty-four months, and went back in to have scar tissue scraped a few times. He also had tubes put into his ears multiple times. There's nothing worse for a mother than seeing your children have surgery. All my boys had surgeries young, but Robbie's were by far the most traumatic for me.

THE COURT TRIAL

Obviously, being a new nursing mother, I had to take the baby to court with me. Robbie was only about six weeks old when we finally got in front of the Judge, to hear the worker's comp case. He had me take the stand and explain what happened, how I fell in the chair, and how the injury occurred. Once I got back to the table with my lawyer, he decided to give me a verbal berating. He stated that "I was what's wrong with this system, if I can't live off the system on welfare, or some other way, I'll try and claim an injury!' I was shocked yet again! Here I am, an injured person, only looking for what's right. I was married, I had worked since I was ten years old, I've never been on welfare, and I'm what's wrong with this system? He denied my claim, refusing to look at my medical records, which clearly showed the ruptured disc, and stated that the legal system in this country was founded on the ability of a Judge to be able to tell if someone was lying! Even if I was a pathological liar and was hit by a car, I would still be injured! Everyone knew he was in the pocket of the insurance companies. I appealed all the way to the Rhode Island Supreme Court, several times, and they refused to hear the appeal each time, based on the Judge calling me a liar. I ended up paying for the surgery when I finally had it by myself.

Years later the judge was up for an appointment to family court. I took three days out of work, unpaid, to testify as to what he said. Of course, the press wanted to know why I was there, and if his testimony was in my transcript, which of course it was. He claimed I was just a disgruntled worker that couldn't collect, and had a vendetta against him. I never got the chance to testify, however. For the entire three days, his ex-wife and children testified that he verbally and physically abused them. Apparently, he drove his daughter to try and commit suicide, never saw his children, and was always late with child support. A real martyr for a family court judge! Needless to say, he did not get the appointment. I ran into him one other time at a political event that I was at with my husband at the time. He walked up next to me at the cheese and cracker table, and it was all I could do not to tell him what I thought of him! He was a slobbering drunk by that point, so he probably wouldn't have remembered anyway!

WHEN THE CHEATING BEGAN

I didn't go back to work outside the house after having the baby; instead I sold Tupperware and was helping my husband at the time with his political aspirations. He was a truck driver when I met him, but he had worked his way up to be the secretary treasurer of the local teamsters union. At one point he had organized the largest union drive in the country, Rhode Island Hospital, and was on the Today show. Some people can't handle fame or money; it all goes to their head. He was one of those people. People change, due to circumstances in their life, and he was not the man I fell in love with and married.

I would make all the food, cater the election events, and cook for the crew when they would come to the house to make signs. He also helped other local politicians work on their election campaigns, so there was always a lot of activity at the house. I had plenty to keep me busy, and things to do to try and save money. He spent it faster than he could make it. I would wash starch and iron his dress shirts instead of using the drycleaner. That was thirty dollars a month in savings. I would spend hours clipping coupons, and see how much I could get off of my food bill. It was like a game for me, I would save hundreds a month! I also had a huge garden that I would freeze the vegetables from, and dry the herbs to make Christmas gifts with. I would cook him a gourmet dinner every night for dinner, since I was a trained chef, and he loved food! I sold so much Tupperware; they wanted to make me a manager! Then I started a fruit and gift basket business from the house, and got orders through the local florists. When I got an order for thirty-five baskets the day I came home from the hospital with the second baby, I realized it was just too much for one person anymore!

I became pregnant with our second son just about two years after the first one was born. I can remember lying on the couch pregnant, waiting for my husband to come rolling in at about four in the morning. He would give me a story telling me he was too drunk to drive home, so he slept in his car. Little did I know he had been cheating on me already! I insisted he go to Alcoholics Anonymous, or the marriage was over. He went, and came home to tell me he's not an alcoholic, but he's a binge drinker, so he can drink socially. Boy, was I naive! It took a few more years before I found out about Al Anon, where families of alcoholics can go, and I decided to get the truth! An alcoholic is an alcoholic! They can't drink, period! The addictions also move around. First for him it was food, then it was work, like when we met, then it was booze, then it was sex, then it was drugs.

I had a second child, another boy, named Ricky, in May of 1989. I still had the back injury, so I spent the last three months of the pregnancy in bed due to the pain. He was a difficult pregnancy due to the injury. He also did a complete turnaround in my belly, the night before I delivered him! His father couldn't handle being in the delivery room. He was the thinnest in his life, because he was actually sticking to the diet I put him on. His weight had ballooned up to three hundred pounds before the diet, because he was going to all the finest restaurants for lunch every day. But being on the diet, he hadn't eaten with me in the hospital, and almost passed out on the floor during the delivery! The baby was face up instead of face down, so I wasn't able to wait for a contraction to try and push him out. By the time he was delivered, I couldn't even move. I wasn't able to have an epidural because of the back injury, and all they could do was give me a shot to take the edge off. They tucked him under my arm, after they checked him out, and sent me off to my room!

My back doctor had been prescribing some pretty strong pain killers and muscle relaxers for me to be able to function. I was getting concerned, because it seemed to me like I was getting addicted to them. I didn't take anything while I was pregnant, which was why it was so difficult. I went for a visit to the back doctor after having the baby, and had another x-ray. He informed me that if I wanted to have any more children, I needed to have back surgery. Otherwise, he said, they're going to be picking pieces of the disc out off my back, because it will explode! So even though I had been putting the surgery off, because I thought I was going to die, I decided I did want to have more children, so we scheduled the surgery. It was scheduled for two weeks before Thanksgiving, in 1990. My mother in-law agreed to stay at the house and help my husband with the children while I was in the hospital. I can remember when it was scheduled, because I still cooked the Thanksgiving Dinner when I came home from the surgery!

WHEN I DIED

I died when I was twenty-seven years old. I knew I was going to die, and put my surgery off for five years, until I had no choice. I just knew if I went in for the surgery I needed, I was absolutely going to die. Of course everyone, including my husband at the time, thought I was just scared, and that it was a normal reaction to the prospect of a serious surgery. The night before my surgery, when they were doing an MRI dye test, I died. I had a severe allergic reaction to the iodine in the dye. I had told them in advance that I thought I was allergic to it, and what my previous reaction was, but they told me that was normal. As soon as they injected the iodine into the IV, I saw the monitor flat line, and I was gone! When I left my body, it wasn't like falling asleep, but more like falling into a little bit of a mist. It didn't hurt at all, in fact I felt nothing! I watched the scene unfolding from the top corner of the hospital room, outside of my body. In the meantime, I heard voices, not just the ones in the room, and around the hospital, but coming from higher up above me. Then my life started to unfold before my eyes. It was almost like a movie reel on fast forward, and I was just observing it. As I was reviewing my life, everyone I ever loved, and every important moment, I started thinking about my two children at the time. Then I heard a voice from above and behind me, and I was told that it wasn't supposed to be my time. I was flying, not floating! I could see not just my room; I could see all the rooms! I could see and hear what everyone was doing in the hospital! I was almost overwhelmed with the feeling of pure love and joy that just kept washing over me in waves! I was told I could stay if I wanted to, or I could go back, it was my choice. I now tried to bring my focus to my body lying on the table below. They had tipped it completely down, with my feet up, and the doctor was slapping my face, and yelling at me! "We can't lose you!" "We can't lose you!" I felt nothing. I wasn't in my body! I had seen the doctor hit the big button on the wall when I first left my body, and a nurse came running in with a crash cart. They were using shock-paddles on my body and trying to get a heart-beat. Then they then injected something into the IV line. I thought about who was going to raise my children if I wasn't there. I thought about how much I loved them and still wanted to see them grow up. I was thinking about everything I had gone through to have them, and how it was one of the greatest joys of my life having them. I was back in my body the instant I made the decision.

When I came back, the doctor told me I was a very lucky lady. He explained that he was a resident at the hospital, and at the end of his month long training. He said if it had been the beginning of the month, he wouldn't have realized it wasn't a normal reaction, and I probably wouldn't have made it. I didn't bother telling him how close I came to staying on the other side. Our souls are all made of pure energy and love, and when you go, the two things you take with you, are your knowledge, and love.

Knowing the things that I know now, I have to laugh! Whoever gave me the choice on the other side knew all along that I was going to choose to come back. They know everything that's going to happen before it happens. They don't always tell us, so they don't influence our free will and our journey, but they know! I still had a lot of important things left to do in my life, including having my youngest son Ryan.

THE HOUSE ON KENWOOD STREET

After being married about four years, we bought a vacant piece of land next to our house and decided to build a bigger one. I handled most of the work as the general contractor to build the new house. We designed it together, and I researched the builder and subcontractors. At the last minute, my husband at the time decided that he didn't want to wait for the builder we wanted to use, and wanted to use a contractor that one of his buddies had recommended. He was adamant that he was a great builder. I told him I wanted to see something that he actually built. We were directed to a plat of new houses, where the guy hung a sign up in the front on a tree, because he knew we were coming. Needless to say, he didn't have a clue how to build a house! After the frame went up, I told my husband he needs to pay attention to the work. There wasn't one board on the house that was square or plumb. The guy and his whole crew were doing drugs on the job, and the building inspector ordered it to be torn down. So much for his buddy!

At the time, we had a homeowner policy on the new house, because we expected to occupy it within six months. There was a clause in the homeowner policy that would pay us in the event of a collapse under construction. If it was left there it would have collapsed on its own, but because the building inspector required it to be torn down, they refused to pay. We had to take the insurance company to court, as well as the builder. There was recent case law in New Jersey and New York that upheld that the insurance company had to pay. Of course, we made case law in Rhode Island, and such is my luck, they found against us and for the insurance company! The lawsuit against the builder didn't go any better.

If I hadn't been good at surviving, we would have lost everything, since we already used most of the money from the construction loan we had taken out. I decided to use credit cards for the difference we lost, and took the house down a board at a time. Most of the lumber was now too short for its original purpose and it made the next contractor's job more expensive, because he now had to work with a lot of used lumber. But I did get the house built.

The lawyer we had hired to handle the lawsuit, Healy apparently had some issues of his own! Every time I would talk to him, he would tell me we had court dates coming up, and then postpone them. At one point he told me we won the case by default, and could expect a check shortly. Then he said they appealed. In the meantime, he would never send me the documentation that I needed. I finally went to the courthouse myself, to find out we had actually lost all the cases due to

our attorney not responding! I called him from the courthouse to tell him I was there and on my way over to his office. When I got to his office, he was pacing the sidewalk back and forth. He took me inside, and at that point my husband arrived. He wanted to know what we planned on doing, and said he would write us a check for ten thousand dollars to take care of it, and he would fix the cases.
(In hindsight we should have taken the check.) We told him that we weren't going to do anything until we spoke to another attorney. The next attorney recommended we file charges against the builder with the attorney general's office and that he would take the cases on and see what he could do about getting them reinstated. The attorney general had a hearing, to sanction Mr. Healy. A female district attorney, Lisi, who later became a judge, told me in advance that he had no prior offenses, and this was the first time he had ever had a problem. Wow, do people lie! The judge opened what he called a "rap sheet" and read all the prior crimes that Healy had already committed! Apparently, he was the son of a family court judge, and had been receiving special treatment! Sometimes I pray Karma catches up fast! By the time the lawsuits got reinstated and wound their way through court, the builder offered $1500 towards all the legal fees we'd already doled out, or he was going to claim bankruptcy and we would get nothing. He didn't have a bond, and his insurance didn't cover his incompetence! Where oh where is the justice! I had nightmares about running into this man for several years. I avoided every restaurant he

worked at. I assume he was as bad a cook as a builder!

ONCE A CHEATER ALWAYS A CHEATER!

After the house was up, my husband, who was not very handy, would stay at home with the kids in the old house, while I worked on the finish work for the new house. I did all the tile work in three full bathrooms and two full kitchens, both floors and walls. We had built the house with an in-law apartment, trying to think ahead. I picked out all the cabinets and wooden stair parts, and stained all of them. I also installed all the doorknobs and cabinet hardware. Little did I know he was on the phone the whole time with the woman he was cheating on me with!

As soon as we sold the old house and moved into the new one, I got pregnant with our third son. At some point, I can remember we had a problem with the chimney leaking when it rained, and I was up on the roof of the house at eight months pregnant with the contractor. My husband didn't like heights! I was also the one climbing the ladder to put up the Christmas lights on the gutters. I did what needed to be done. Lesson learned, now I won't touch a screwdriver if I have a guy around to help!

He had made a lot of enemies during his time in politics, and there were also union members that didn't want to see him re-elected. One night around midnight, we heard this horrendous crash, and were awoken from a sound sleep. I went to the front of the house, and a huge trapezoid window we had over the foyer and been shot out! There was glass everywhere! I spent the night cleaning it all up. When the kids got up in the morning, we told then a bird flew into it, so they weren't scared. Robbie found the only piece of glass I missed, when he put his hand on the stair railing to walk down, and cut his hand. I was also being followed by people when I took the kids to and from preschool. I don't know if it was just to try and scare me, or if they planned on trying to hurt me or the children. It seemed I didn't have a lot of pleasant relaxing times.

When I was about seven months pregnant, my husband at the time told me he had to stay overnight for the driving school he was teaching at, out of town. I had no reason not to believe him. He was going out of town about once every other week. One night when he was gone, the water bed we slept in let go, and I woke up soaked in water! Of course I had to drag the whole thing to the street because he didn't get home until around midnight every night. A few weeks later, I started passing a kidney stone. If you've ever had one, it's worse pain then delivering a baby! I also had the other two kids at home, and no one to watch them. I couldn't reach my husband, because unbeknownst to me, he was with his mistress and had his phone shut off. By the time my neighbors got home to watch the kids and take me to the hospital, I was in labor. I still couldn't reach my husband until he decided to troll in around ten o'clock that night. I don't know what I would have done without the neighbors! One neighbor watched the kids, and her husband drove me to the hospital. They stopped the labor, and I passed one kidney stone. They put a steint in to keep the channel open between my bladder and my kidney. I went home the next day, but I still had another kidney stone. I was bleeding so much, and was in so much pain from it scraping my kidney. I told them they had to take it out. Unfortunately, when they did, I started to pass the second kidney stone! Again, I had no husband and no one to help me with the other two children except for the neighbors. I was in excruciating pain at home, passing another kidney stone.

I truly thought he was working hard for his family. I trusted everything he told me, and never questioned it. It wasn't that I was naive; it was that I was trustworthy, and I had no reason at that time to believe he wasn't. In later years, I would come to learn that he was a narcissist, and he felt the world really traveled around him.

AGING PARENTS

I would bring my children to visit my father about once a month so that they would have some idea of what normal families do. We never stayed long, however, since we always visited in his office. The highlight of the visit for them was getting donuts from the donut shop! My father had an apartment upstairs from his office, with his disabled wife Nancy. She would lie in bed and watch television all day. She was mentally ill with multiple sclerosis that had hit her brain stem, and she was completely disabled. He knew she had it when he married her, at about the age of thirty. They had quite the age difference; he was about thirty years older than her! He would go up and feed her, and change her diaper, and check on her a few times a day. He didn't want to put her in a nursing home because of the expense. He would never let me upstairs, obviously because he didn't want me to see the conditions they were living in. He didn't bathe her, or change the bed they both slept in, and apparently had given himself a hernia trying to move her at one point.

My Father's Injury

As my father aged, I would call him every day just to check on him, like any good daughter would. On one occasion, I called, and he was lying in the parking lot of the business waiting for an ambulance with my brother Albert. He had tripped and fallen, and broken his femur bone. I asked my brother to make sure that they take him to Rhode Island Hospital, since they had a state-of-the-art trauma unit. It was a ten-minute ride, but across the state line. I could hear him asking the ambulance driver, who refused. I asked him to hand the phone to the driver, so I could talk to him. The driver's response to me was that they were taking him to Attleboro, unless I wanted to call a private ambulance, but it was raining out, and he would hate to see an eighty-year-old man left lying on the ground in the rain! He then hung up on me! I called my brother back, and told him I would meet him in Attleboro. When I arrived at the emergency room, I asked to have him transported to Rhode Island Hospital, and asked what the procedure was. I was told that I had to get a physician at Rhode Island Hospital to be willing to accept him before they would transfer him. I called and pleaded with the emergency room there. They agreed to take him, and I called a private ambulance company. It was a long day, and by the time they got him there, it was late on a Friday afternoon.

I spoke with the orthopedic doctor that reviewed him, who told us about a new surgery that only he and one other doctor had been doing in the country! Instead of cutting his hip open, they were making a tiny incision just above the knee and another in the thigh. Then they inserted a supportive rod through his bone for support. We opted to have the surgeon we were speaking with do the surgery, rather than waiting four days more for the more experienced doctor to return from a trip and do it. The surgery was a success, and he was sent to a nursing home for a six-week recovery period. Of course I was criticized by my older brother Arthur, and younger brother William, since the nursing home wasn't in their back yard! They all went to visit him once during his stay. I was there, as were my children, sometimes twice a day. Afterwards, he had no limp, and didn't need the use of a cane to walk.

I filed a complaint with the city in regards to the ambulance driver, and let them know how ironic it was, that the person responsible for the majority of the funding of the department, due to the amount of money the city got from his lottery sales, was completely neglected, and it could have potentially cost him his life! They begged me not to pursue it further, and claimed that the ambulance driver had been on the fire department for almost twenty years, and that they would internally reprimand him. I left it in their hands. I always believe that Karma takes care of things the way that it should.

Moving Nancy to a Nursing Home

In the meantime, I had to go upstairs with the intention of seeing what care his disabled wife Nancy needed. She never liked me. She was close to my sister Shirley, but she was always pretty nasty to me. At one point when I was around twelve years old, she walked up to me in the parking lot of the donut shop, and pulled my tube top down, calling me a slut for wearing it, and completely exposed my breasts to everyone I was around!

I hadn't actually seen her in about fifteen years, and had no idea what to expect. Well, she was about two hundred and fifty pounds, and was lying in the bed in a dirty diaper, and the bed completely covered with items! There were no sheets on the mattress, and it was black and smelly. The apartment was covered in garbage, dirty diapers, and half-eaten food. There was an open thirty-gallon garbage can overflowing, and there were so many fruit flies that I had to leave and get a face mask to go back in. I also got my brother Albert to go in with me. He apparently was aware that the apartment was bad, but even he wasn't aware of just how bad it was. He basically tried to avoid any confrontation with our dad. My father was stubborn, and did what he wanted to do, the hell with everyone and everything else! Hence the reason he had Nancy there and not in a nursing home he didn't want to spend the money. I asked Nancy if she could stand, and she said yes, so I tried to lift her to stand and get into the wheelchair that was there. She couldn't stand! In fact I almost ended up putting myself in the hospital trying to help her! I told my brother that we needed to get her out of there, because no one should be in those conditions. I rented an apartment down the street, and got some furniture so that she and my father could live there when he got out of the nursing home. Again, it was all at my expense, the rent, the security deposit and the furniture. We were able to get Nancy down the back staircase, in the wheelchair, and into the bed in the apartment, with the help of some very strong men! Then all she did was start screaming! She had the mentality of a five-year-old girl, and wanted to know where my father was. She was afraid to be alone. I certainly couldn't stay with her; I had three children and two businesses to run! After being advised by social services to take her to a hospital for evaluation, I ended up calling an ambulance to get her to a hospital, and get her checked out medically and mentally.

There was absolutely no way my father could or should have been trying to take care of her by himself. From the hospital, she ended up being moved to a nursing home, where she still resides. Sadly, she never had any children, or siblings, and her parents are both long deceased, so my father was her only visitor.

In the meantime, my brother ordered a dumpster, and proceeded to clean out and gut the apartment my father had been living in with her. He refurnished it, and made it completely handicap accessible for my father. My father stayed in the apartment I had rented for him and his wife for about two months, and then moved back into the apartment above the bakery. Of course, when he left, he gave no notice, and left all the furniture there, so the landlord ended up taking me to court for the additional money. My father couldn't have cared less! He was completely ungrateful for anything that I or my brother had done to help him and his wife. Instead, he was angry, claiming that we meddled in his living conditions. We did explain to him, that if the Board of Health had ever seen the conditions he was living in, they would have shut down his donut making operation, since the bakery was just down stairs!

Years later he admitted, that his primary care physician told him, that if I hadn't gotten him to Rhode Island Hospital for the minimally invasive surgery he had, he would not have survived. He already had advances prostate cancer, and the beginnings of bladder cancer.

My Father's Illusion

My father was very wealthy. He had a very lucrative business and was the largest single lottery dealer in the state of Massachusetts for many years. He would never spend any money on himself however, or ever offer to help me. Since the time I was nineteen or twenty, I had been buying all of his cloths for him. Socks, underwear, even taking him to buy shoes! Of course, he would never offer to pay me back, and I would never ask. I didn't believe it was right if I was able to afford it. Not that I was rich, I had three kids, and worked part time jobs in the home while I was married. He always claimed he had no money! I would believe it as well, since he was supporting everyone else!

He would send $100 a week to my mother, and once in a while help her out on her rent, and always complain. I would remind him, that she was entitled to half of what they owned, including the business when they divorced, and she took nothing! Not one red cent! He would then stop complaining. Many times he was going to stop sending her any money, all she had was social security, and I would have to again remind him. He had no problem however supporting Shirley, William, William Jr. and even grossly overpaying my brother Albert. For the most part, my father made it clear that women had zero value other than servicing men and having babies. The males in the family held all the value to him, since they carried the family name forward. But the reality was that without me, he would have lost his business several times over!

At one point, he was nine years behind on his taxes, because his previous accountant had a flood in his office, and all the records for the company that year had been destroyed. I spent a year paying for a babysitter, and going to his office to rebuild the records for him to move forward and catch up on the taxes. He did not offer to compensate me. On another occasion, they were threatening to put a tax lien on his property, and I got a mortgage for him on his mixed-use property for him to pay back the taxes. Then he insisted my brother Albert by a three-family tenement that abutted the donut shop, in the hopes of expanding someday. It was a short sale, and there was no time to get a mortgage. My husband at the time, Bill, agreed for us to let Albert borrow the money from a line of credit we had, until he could apply for a mortgage to pay us back.

Through the years, I really had no contact with my mother, other than when she occasionally came to the house for the holidays, which I always invited her for. She felt awkward and mostly kept to herself. There was a time, however, when she would stop by my daycare in Massachusetts to say hello. On one of those occasions, I had to ask her a question. I wanted to know why she hadn't protected us from my father, since she had to have known what was going on. I felt horrible after for asking. She was about seventy-five at the time, and she broke down in tears. She said that she felt she had no choice. If she had called the authorities, they would have put us all in separate foster homes, because she had no money to support us, and he would have been in jail. She didn't know what to do at the time.

It's funny however, as horrible as my father had been to her when they were married, she called him every day in later years, and when they were both at my home for the holidays, they would sit and chat like they were still a married couple.

THE FIRST DIVORCE

At the time, my husband was working as the secretary treasurer of the local teamsters union, and claimed he was teaching a CDL driving school at the local college. I had no reason not to believe him. He was the person that started the driving school. There was another election coming up, and I had been busy taking care of the three boys, and making the food for the party. The baby was about six weeks old. One of my girlfriends was at the house helping me make meatballs, and she commented, "I don't know how you do it all by yourself, if it was my husband, I'd think he was cheating on me." I'll never forget my reply. "You don't understand, he would never do that to me, and I would never do that to him!" We love each other too much! The seed was planted though, and my intuition kicked in. I started to think about when he was out nights, and what he would say his reasons were. I took out the mobile phone bill. Back in those days, mobile phones were rare. They were a phone in a bag, and very expensive. The bills detailed every call that was made or received. I started to call some of the numbers that were listed. I figured if he was cheating on me, then he would be calling her. There were a lot of nursing home numbers on the bill. I figured one of two things was happening, either he was organizing a nursing home, or he was seeing a nurse! He walked in the door on that Friday night about 11:30; I had just finished washing the kitchen floor. I looked at him coming up the stairs, and asked him point blank if he was cheating on me. He immediately went into defensive mode! “I don’t know who called and told you that, but they’re lying,” he said. I very calmly told him that no one called me. I then asked him why he was calling nursing homes. They say people want to get caught, I don’t know. He spilled the beans himself, and then couldn’t stop telling me! He was seeing a nurse. He had been seeing her for a couple of years now, and claims he met her the night he rolled in with me pregnant on the couch with the second child. Then he went on to make me feel sorry for the girl, telling me how he never took her out in public because he didn’t want to be seen with her. Then he told me she spent a lot of money on a gold bracelet for him for Christmas, that he told me the guys pitched in and bought a thank you gift. He went on to tell me she had been addicted to cocaine, and he helped her get over the habit. That was a lie, they were both using it. Having never tried it myself, I didn’t know what to look for.

That Sunday, as he went to his union meeting, I decided to call her, apologize for his behavior, and ask where I could send the bracelet back to. She was shocked when she answered the phone and heard me! He had told her I was in a mental hospital, and that he lived in the house with his mother and the kids. He told her the third baby was an accident, conceived on a "conjugal visit!" "In fact," she said, "he comes here every Sunday morning, and should be here any minute, hang on." Then she handed him the phone. I felt like a fool! I fell for the story he fed me. He had no intention of breaking off the relationship in fact, when he came back that day, he had three garbage bags full of clothes that were at her house. It looked like he had moved out already!

Easter was the following Sunday. I was sitting at the kitchen table with my mother-in-law, whom I had told about the affair, when the girl showed up at my door with a two-year-old in tow. I have no idea why! I think she just wanted to see for herself that he was lying to her as well. Seeing the age of the child, I had to ask him if he was the father. He said he wasn't, and said the father was in prison for selling drugs. No surprise there! It's funny how you find out the things you need to know at the right time in your life. Had I found out he had been cheating earlier, we wouldn't have had our third son, Ryan. Life is all about divine timing.

I was devastated when I found out he had been cheating on me, and for so long. I was still dealing with the hormone changes from pregnancy as well. I had trouble functioning on an everyday level, like feeding the baby or kids, because all I could do was cry. I called my doctor, who ended up putting me on medication, so I could at least sleep. Thank God I had wonderful neighbors at the time, because they were the ones feeding the baby and helping me to get the others dressed and fed as well.

We were trying to work out what had happened, and took a family vacation to New Hampshire to try and reconnect. I remember him telling me that he didn't love me anymore, and he loved her instead, but that he would try and make it work because of the kids. I was devastated all over again! When we got home the next day, I made dinner, and had a few glasses of wine with the medication I was on. I started to convince myself that maybe my kids would be better off with him and her. I went into the bathroom with the phone and called my closest friend at the time, Nancy. I was crying, and told her that I loved her, and I just wanted to say goodbye. I then put the phone down, leaving it off the hook. I went into the safe, took out the 22 handgun, and told my husband I was going for a drive. Thankfully, Nancy knew what I was planning. When she couldn't call the house phone back, she called the police. They sent one car to the house to ask my husband what I was driving, and other officers were looking for me. I went to the ocean, since I've always been drawn to it. I wasn't afraid to die, I already did, and it was beautiful there. I was just getting ready to write a suicide note, and say goodbye to my children, when the police showed up. They asked me what I was doing. I said that I was just watching the water. They asked if I was going to kill myself, and I guess I either didn't answer fast enough, or didn't answer at all. They asked me how, and again I said I didn't know. They said I needed to come with them. They never searched me, but I had the gun in my skirt pocket. They took me to the hospital, where my husband and mother-in-law were already waiting. I told my husband I had the gun in my pocket, and I didn't want them to find it, or I knew they would want to commit me for a thirty-day observation. I went into the bathroom and put it behind the toilet, and he went in to retrieve it. Since I had no note, and they couldn't figure out how I was going to do it, they released me.

I now know that suicide is never an acceptable option to leave this world. It's like quitting the "game of life." and leaving everyone you were supposed to interact with hanging! People that commit suicide have a lot of work to do on the other side, because they let a lot of people down. If not for being so impaired by drugs and alcohol, I don't believe I ever would have considered it, even though I had never felt such pain before in my life.

We went through marriage counseling for months, and when he thought it was all better, wanted to have another baby. I guess he figured that if I was pregnant I'd stay busy and he could go back to life with the side chick as usual. I knew he hadn't stopped seeing her. She knew that I knew where she lived, so she moved and changed her phone number. Back then, people had pagers instead of cell phones. If someone wanted to talk to you, they would page you, and you would return the call. You could also send a short text message. I went to the pager store, and told them that my husband was out of town, and I needed to get a clone of his pager, so I could return the business calls. The first thing I got was her new phone number. From there, I had a friend on the police force run the number to get her new home address. Next, I called a babysitter, and asked if I could borrow her car. I drove to the girlfriends new house around lunchtime. Just as I pulled up in front of her house, a car pulled up alongside of me in the opposite direction, with a co-worker of my husband driving. My husband walked out of her front door, walked in front of the car I was driving, got into the other car, and then realized it was me that was driving, and that I had just caught him red handed! That was it for me! But easier said than done!

Divorce is a long drawn out process, and the only people that make any money are the lawyers. We tried staying in the house together, with him living in the in-law apartment, but it didn't work. Every time I went out with my girlfriends, he would come home and accuse me of cheating on him! At one point he started to get violent, and I had to call the police to have him removed from the house.

The next thing he did was take ten thousand dollars from a line of credit that we had, even though we both agreed not to touch it. He bought himself all new furniture and moved into an apartment in Providence. He wasn't paying me child support, and I had no income, so I had to find a way to pay the bills. I took a job during the day as a private duty CNA for an elderly couple while the kids were in school. I also worked two nights a week overnight at my dad's donut shop again. My girlfriend Nancy would sleep overnight with the kids so I could work, and I would come home in time to get them off to school. I can remember on more than one occasion, driving home in the morning, and falling asleep at the wheel. I woke up once in head on traffic! Even when I finally got him into court and they ordered him to pay child support, all the checks he would give me came back for non-sufficient funds. He also wasn't paying the mortgage on the house. I rented out the in-law unit to a young couple to help with the bills. I went to try and apply for welfare, and was turned down, because I owned a house. I couldn't believe it! I had three children to feed, and no money, and they could care less! I was grateful I was able to find work as quickly as I did.

I finally sold the house, and ended up moving into a house in Rehoboth with the kids for the school system. One night I was in bed with the kids reading a bed time story and the phone rang. It was their father calling. Apparently, he was out of town in Washington with a married woman, and he "butt dialed" my phone number! For the next thirty minutes, I recorded the conversation going back and forth between them, until they started having sex. Then I shut off the recorder and hung up the phone. I called him back and left a message, for him to check the last phone call on his phone, and I informed him that I had recorded the entire event. The next day, he flew to my house from the airport, to find out what my intention was with the recording. I told him that he needed to stop fighting me for custody of the kids so he doesn't have to pay child support, because there wasn't a judge out there that would let someone with such low moral standards raise three boys! He agreed to back off of wanting full custody. He had free legal services as part of his benefit package, so he did whatever he wanted, and just dragged it out in court, figuring I would just give up.

* * *

Finally into Court

When we finally got into court for the divorce, I was so tired of dealing with him. I just wanted it over with. My lawyer was supposed to be there at nine in the morning, and did not show until one in the afternoon. He then informed me after two-and- a-half years of waiting for a court date, that he's not ready for a trial and it's going to have to be postponed again. I lost it! I informed him that if he isn't ready for a trial, he's fired! I'll represent myself, because I was not leaving that courthouse that day without being divorced. At that moment, the Judge was walking by. He came over and assumed I was upset because the lawyer was four hours late. I said "No, I'm upset because it's been two and a half years, and knowing that we were scheduled for trial he still isn't ready and wants to postpone again!" The Judge turned to the lawyer and told him he better get ready, because it is going to trial right now! That lawyer didn't represent me well. I had no idea what I was giving up when I gave up my pension and social security rights, and I was so mad I agreed to it. No input from the lawyer at all. They put me on the stand, and asked if I told my husband that if I wanted to, I would go screw a football team. I told the judge I did say that, after I caught him cheating on me with the same girl for about three years. The judge had heard enough, and granted the divorce. I had to have it ordered that the child support come out of his check and get paid through the state however, since his checks were never any good and always late.

He went downhill even further after that. I sold the house and moved to Rehoboth for a better school system. My oldest son was special needs. He had ADD and learning disabilities. Rehoboth was the number one school in the state at the time for special needs children. I no sooner moved, we had been divorced about three months, when he pulled up to the house to pick up the kids up for his weekend. He came to the door and told me he wants me to know he just got married! I didn't even know what to say! Now I had no health insurance either! He only had to cover me until either one of us remarried. He married a stripper that he met in a strip club! He brought her to the Health and Welfare Meeting in Florida, and married her in front of a captive audience during lunch! I had friends that were there, and they had no notice as to what was happening. They actually thought it was a comedy show! It lasted six weeks, and he had it annulled, but not before she stole all his credit cards, and wrote bad checks around town. He had to resign his board of director position at the credit union, because that's where the checks were drawn.

While he was with her however, one of my children got injured. He left her to watch the kids while he went to go out somewhere. She also had his phone. I think she wasn't quite stable, and took the phone on purpose. She would call me from it, whenever she got the chance, and taunt me, telling me that she would get his life insurance, and other weird things. That morning she called me from his phone again, and said one of the kids was hurt. I asked where their father was, and she wouldn't tell me. Knowing that she's not all there, I didn't know if she was taunting me again, or if it was true. I asked to talk to my son. She handed him the phone, and he started crying, telling me he hurt his leg and he can't walk. I told him to tell his brothers to get ready; I was coming to pick them up. He lived in Providence at this time, renting an apartment from our friend that owned the motorcycle shop. When I got there, I rang the front doorbell. I could see my other two children looking out the window at me on the second floor. She opened the door slightly, and said, "You can't come in here. I just called the police." I pushed the door open and ran up the stairs to my son. He was in the middle of a big landing area at the top of the stairs and couldn't walk. Apparently, he was climbing up the inside of the doorway, like a spider, and fell. I told the other two kids to follow me, and I carried him down the stairs. When I got to the bottom, the police were just arriving. They wanted to know who I was and what was going on. I explained that these are my children, my son is injured, and I'm taking him to the hospital. If they want to talk to me they can talk to me there, and I left! Mama lion was coming out again! My son had the tendon torn off of the back of his leg. It's a very painful and long healing injury. Sadly, their father's negligence continued throughout the years.

RAISING MY CHILDREN ALONE

I was alone raising my children after my first divorce, for about ten years. I have three boys, all about two and a half years apart. Their names are Robbie, Ricky, and Ryan. The three R's! They are by far my greatest accomplishments in this lifetime. It was a tough road raising them alone. Many times I felt like there wasn't enough of me to give after working all day in not one, but usually two businesses. With no one else helping, and the child support either spotty or non-existent, I wanted a better life for my children than I had. The same thing most parents say that grew up in less than stellar conditions.

My oldest son Robbie was the sole survivor of the triplet pregnancy. I can only assume it had something to do with his disabilities. He was a special needs child growing up, with learning disabilities in reading and math, also with comprehension, and retention problems. He did an extra year of preschool, and he stayed back in first grade as well. From there, I paid for private tutors during the summertime to try and keep him up in school. I would work with him constantly, and due to the school system he was in when we lived in Rhode Island, he actually regressed during kindergarten. He entered knowing how to read and write his name, address, and phone number, and by the time he was done that year, he didn't have a clue! I would constantly get phone calls about what he was bringing for snack, not about his education! More often than not, the children would be on the playground while the teacher was cleaning up the classroom from an unruly child that had decimated it!

At one point, his younger brother Ricky, who tested out with a genius IQ at twelve, came home with a D on his test paper. There was a note attached from the teacher, saying she has no idea what happened, because she knows that he knew all the correct answers. When I asked Ricky what happened, he told me that he wanted to see what happened if he came home with a bad paper. He said Robbie gets all the attention because he needs help all the time. I felt bad, because in a way he was right. Ricky was also the middle child, and they always seem to be the ones that feel left out. He learned very quickly however that he would never do that on a test again. When his quarterly report card came out, they averaged his tests, and he didn't have an A in the class! He wasn't happy!

We moved a few times to accommodate Robbie's educational needs. I had them in private schools until they were unable to meet Robbie's individual educational plan. We started out in the West Bay, and ended up in the East Bay Christian Academies. I would drive about thirty minutes in the morning and afternoon just to get them to school. I also have a medical condition called irritable bowel syndrome that was not under control at the time. It was all I could do to make a thirty-minute drive twice a day, and not have to use a bathroom! Many times, I had to make an emergency bathroom stop at a gas station and haul all the kids in with me or risk an accident!

We then moved to Rehoboth Mass, because they were the number one public school in the northeast for special needs children. At one point I got a phone call from the principal of the school regarding Robbie's storytelling and lies. Apparently, he was telling kids that his mother grew up in a mansion that his grandfather owned, and that he went shopping with George Lucas's kids when they were filming a movie, and saw Robin Williams snorting cocaine. I had to explain that they weren't tall tales, they were true. My kids lived a very strange life due to their father's job and connections.

I enrolled Robbie in a double English class there for all the years he was in junior high school. By the time he got to high school, he was reading on a college level. He still is an adult today with ADD, but he learned wonderful tools to manage it, and is a hard-working family man now.

There were also issues, though, as they got older. Robbie would sneak out when we were sleeping to meet girls, or tell me he was staying at his fathers, and tell his father he was staying with me. He hoped we wouldn't check, but I always did and caught him! His father would also regale the kids with his stories of stealing things from companies that he was working for through the union. For this reason,

Robbie thought it was completely justified to steal from people and companies. He was caught on multiple times stealing from me. First from the piggybank we were saving our change in, a bankbook I had money in for him, and finally my pocketbook. Then he stole all of his brother Ricky's money he was saving. That was just the beginning. He got caught stealing from a couple of jobs, and one decided to prosecute! He made a deal for restitution, and his mother in law signed for a loan for him, because I refused. It took him many years to unlearn what his father taught him, and it ended up costing him a lot of good paying jobs. I believe he's honest now, but it was a long road for him!

Ricky decided to ride Robbie's mini bike in the front yard of our house on Bay State Road in Rehoboth, and hit the stone wall on the edge of the property. The handlebars went into his chest, and could have potentially ruptured his heart. I had to take them all to Hasbro Children's Hospital to get him looked at; it was advised that I not wait for an ambulance, because there might not be time!

Then Ryan had his moments. He was apparently getting picked on when he was in elementary school. He told the kids at the lunch table that he was going to come back with his mother's gun and shoot them if they didn't leave him alone! Thank God the principal was a reasonable man, and didn't suspend him! Now he would have been expelled! Then when he was in high school, I noticed my new bottle of Vodka, that I used to make Vanilla with, was half empty. I asked all of the kids if they knew why, and let them know how concerned I was that one of them was drinking. I honestly thought it was Robbie, since he was already seventeen. It ended up being Ryan that was taking it! A couple of the kids were bullying him again, and they would walk around the football games after school drinking water bottles full of vodka! He told them if they left him alone, he would fill the bottles for them. I explained to him the legal implications of something happening with the kids, and the alcohol coming from our home. He didn't do that anymore! I have to give him credit for being creative with the bullies, however.

As quiet and well behaved as Ricky was, he also had a mischievous side. I remember I received a call from Ryan's school principal after their father had taken them to a school dance on his scheduled weekend to have the kids. The principal informed me that my son Ricky had vandalized his classic car the night of the school dance. I asked him if he was somehow mistaken, because Ricky didn't go to that school, and he must mean Ryan. He stated that Ricky was seen by other children vandalizing his car, by pouring a milkshake or something on the driver's side door. He said he had no idea why he would do it, since they didn't even know each other. I told him I would look into it and get back in touch with him. Sure enough, it was Ricky! When I asked him why, he said he wanted to look "cool" in front of the other kids. I brought him to the school the next morning to apologize to the principal, and offer to wash his car on the following weekend.

Ricky also had an incident when he was in high school as well, that almost cost him an appointment to the Air Force Academy. He was sitting in the library with his class, doing his work and minding his own business. A classmate got up and punched him in the side of the head, knocking him off his chair, and started beating him on the floor. The teacher was in the hallway chatting with another teacher, and wasn't paying attention. Ricky pushed the kid off of him, and was suspended! When I spoke to the principal, he informed me that it was school policy, because Ricky put his hands on him to push him off, he had to be suspended as well. I was fuming! I informed him that I have always taught my children to defend themselves if need be, but from now on, I'll tell them to kick the other kids ass! He just looked at me not knowing what to say! When Ricky applied for the Air Force Academy however, they refused to believe that any education system would be as ignorant as to have a policy where you were suspended for protecting yourself, and thought Ricky was at fault and lying. The principal had to send a letter explaining, that Ricky was telling the truth, and had done nothing to instigate the attack. In fact, the child that attacked him had done it to other kids previously.

Being boys, one by one as they reached puberty, thought they would see if they could rule the house. Each one tried to threaten or push me, since they were so much bigger, and I made it very clear that they were the child and I was the one in charge! Eventually they learned to help, and always respect me.

The Haunted Houses

We lived in three different houses when we were in Rehoboth. The first was a rental property on Route 44. There were only two bedrooms, and not enough space for all the items in the house, so I rented a storage container. I had the three boys sleeping in one room, and I was in the other. We definitely weren't living alone though! We would always hear scratching on the ceiling in the bathroom and my bedroom. We assumed it was a squirrel on the roof or in a crawl space. We would all see a large black shadow figure walk through the apartment during the night. The kids assumed it was me, and I assumed it was Robbie going to the kitchen at night! Needless to say, it was neither! One night I watched it walk through a closed door and into the hallway. We never used the front hallway, but we could always hear footsteps going back and forth. I had bought a Black Hills gold thumb ring when I had taken the kids to New Hampshire on vacation. I would wear it every day, and then put it on my bureau at night when I took my jewelry off. One morning it wasn't there. It had mysteriously disappeared! I had picked up Chinese food a few days later, and we were sitting at the kitchen table. I asked the kids if by chance any of them had seen it, and told them it was missing, when suddenly the light over the table got a surge of electricity and all the light bulbs broke all over our food! Needless to say, we weren't happy!

The next house on Bay State Road used to be the depot station, where families would park their horse and buggy in the olden days, and take the trolley into Providence. It was also the first town office for the town of Rehoboth. When we got it, the house needed a lot of work. I repainted and redid all the hardwood floors. I also had a half bath put in on the first floor, and turned the old 1950's kitchen into a laundry and family room. I made most of my money by buying houses and rehabbing them. The first night in the house, I went to take a bath and all the water came through the downstairs ceiling and onto the floor. The previous owner had tried to do a pluming repair with cheap plastic, a newspaper, and a brick! He had been a truck driver that had cheated on his wife. He moved out with his girlfriend, and didn't pay the health insurance for his wife. She ended up with cancer; she was the school lunch lady in town. His girlfriend threw him out, and when he moved back into the house, he told everyone it was out of the kindness of his heart to take care of his dying wife! She died on the livingroom couch.

The house had many spirits living in it, not just hers! When Robbie moved into his bedroom, he had a black light. When he turned it on, you could see a pentagram on the wall coming through the fresh coat of paint. His daughter was a Wiccan, and I believe she opened a portal. We would have the televisions and radios turn on at all hours of the day and night. The basement light would always be on. We could see it on from the driveway, and if I sent one of the kids to turn it off, it would snap back before we could even back out of the driveway!

One night I was alone in the house and getting ready for bed. I had a Miniature Pinscher dog named Minnie that would sleep in the bed with me every night. This night she stood by the side of the bed with all her hair standing on end. I suddenly heard a man and a woman arguing outside the bedroom door at the bottom of the attic stairs. I called my girlfriend Nancy on the phone, held it out, and asked her if she could hear anything. She asked me what was going on, and wanted to know if the kids were arguing. I explained that they were at their father's and I was alone in the house, and that was going on outside my bedroom door! She asked me if I was going to get up and look, and I said no way! I told her I was going to talk to her until I fell asleep or they stopped arguing! I don't remember which came first anymore. When it came time to sell, I had difficulty because it was so close to the street. I ended up renting it to a local man that was going through a divorce himself, and was going to be moving back into his own house after the divorce. When I went to collect the rent one day, he asked told me to “get in here!” He said, “This place is haunted!” “Do you see those chairs right there?”, as he pointed to some barrel type chairs around his dining room table. “I know I was drunk last night, but I wasn’t that drunk. I woke up to three of those around my bed this morning!” I didn’t know what to say! I just said that I never had a problem! He moved out about two months later. After I sold the house, the new owners pulled up alongside of me at a red light. They asked if I could stop by the house. When I got out of my car and commented on how nice the house looked, the husband didn’t skip a beat when he asked me if the house was haunted. I said I had no idea, and asked him what happened. He refused to say, and I refused to admit anything!

The other house that we lived in was rented, and we would hear banging on the kitchen floor all the time. Apparently the house was built on top of a foundation from a previous house. It had a staircase in the basement that led to nothing. It was a challenge trying to explain these events away so the kids didn’t get scared. We’d also see black shadow people walk around the living room and kitchen area. I didn’t realize they were always there, it was just that I could see them.

Growing Up and Moving Out

One by one, when they turned eighteen, the kids all moved in with their father, or in Ricky's case went to the Air Force Academy. There were no rules and no supervision at their father's house. Robbie was bringing young girls to his house and got one pregnant. She was fifteen at the time, and later became his wife. Ryan started to dabble in drugs when he would be there on the weekends, and I hit the roof when I found out. I figured if he had enough money to buy drugs to use with his son, then he could pay the back child support he owed me. It was somewhere around one hundred and fifty thousand dollars. He was receiving eighty-four thousand dollars a year in pensions and social security disability for alcoholism. He refused to pay, and ended up overnight in jail twice. He then offered Ryan the child support check of eight hundred dollars a month if he moved in with him when he turned eighteen. He thought he was being slick. Instead, what do you think a child is going to do with eight hundred dollars when you just got him hooked on drugs? He went out and bought some! He bought the designer drugs that they were selling at the head shops as bath salts. They sent him into a psychotic break! He was roaming the streets for three days before he was found. I got him into the local private mental hospital to get him some help, but he was so brainwashed from his father it was horrible! He told me his father had no money, (which he never did because he spends it on drugs), and that it was my fault because I was making him pay the child support. I made an agreement to take a life insurance policy on his father instead of the money, so it didn't hinder Ryan's recovery, and eventually he'll see that his father will still have no money. In the meantime, his father bought him a one way-ticket to an alcohol rehab facility in Florida that he had been in, and shipped Ryan off alone in the condition he was in. He refused to tell me where he had sent him, only he and his family knew. He also lied to me and said he did not have him travel alone in his condition. All I knew was my son was in trouble, his father is and was a jack ass, and I needed to find him!

I spent a month faxing letters out to every hospital and rehab facility there was in Florida. At the end of the month, I received a phone call. The man said he was a nurse at a facility that had my son, and that he could lose his job for calling me, since it's a violation of the HIPPA laws. He said he had to call in good conscience, because if I didn't get him right away, he was going to be released to the street, and would be dead in no time! He said that he had been put in an alcohol recovery facility, and he was on drugs that caused a psychotic break. They were not equipped to handle his condition, and he was now in his third state hospital! I planned on flying down on the weekend to bring him back and was trying to get everything lined up at the business. He called me again to tell me there wasn't enough time, they were releasing him. I needed to send a plane ticket for him, and he would make sure he got on the plane safely; I just needed to meet the plane here. I got him back into the original hospital he was in before his father "stole" him. He ended up getting the help he needed, however he was still very heavily under his father's influence. When he was discharged, he again wanted to go live with his father. After having to "take care" of him for a few years, and not being able to have his own life, he finally moved out on his own.

His father's family is so dysfunctional, that when my ex-father-in - law passed away, they had him cremated without even informing Ricky. They had no service for him. They then took his ashes to the cemetery, dug a hole with a shovel, and dumped the ashes in! Again, without saying anything, because they didn't want to spend the money to open the grave. I can just imagine what they did with the life insurance money!

For his whole life, Ryan had been trying to get his father's love and attention. Even when he was with the children, their father would ignore them. He would bring them with him to the union hall, and they would hang around with all the guys. They picked up quite a vocabulary! He also spent their entire life telling them lies about me, like I cheated on him! He is a classic narcissist, he is the most important thing, and the world revolves around him! Ryan took it the hardest when we split up, since he was only ten months old. His father would constantly make plans to see him, and then not show at the last minute, usually because he either had a date, or was going out of town. Ryan would always get angry and take it out on me. At one point when he was about nine, I finally had enough, and told him that he needs to pay attention to who he is directing his anger at. I am not the person that's always letting him down; I'm the person that is always there for him. He understood, but it was terrible to see him always so disappointed.

At one point their father was going to take them to Florida for a week, after he married the drug addict he had been cheating on me with. He married her a few years after our divorce, and wasn't able to divorce her until she ended up in prison. They threw a New Year's party to get people there, and got married. At the last minute he decided that he wasn't going to give me any information as to where the children would be. I was not letting them go if I didn't know where. In hindsight, I think he was going to try and keep them in Florida, thus circumventing the child support law again. He never thought far enough ahead to understand it would have been kidnapping! Again, he told the children it was my fault, I wouldn't let them go. He didn't mention that he refused to tell me where they were going.

Eating Addictions

I always thought it was important to have dinner as a family every night, so that's what we did. As soon as I got home at night, I made sure they had a good meal on the table for dinner as a family, and we would talk about how our day went. At one point in time I noticed the little one, Ryan, who was around eleven at the time, kept leaving the table in the middle of dinner to go to the bathroom. He would then come back to the table and have another full meal! He was always a little chubby as a child, and loved food like his father. His father had always been overweight as well. By the third time I caught on and asked him if he was O.K. He admitted that he was going into the bathroom, and making himself vomit, so he could eat more food, because it tasted so good! After I explained the dangers to him, and that it was the beginning of an eating disorder, he stopped. He was always a little on the chubby side as a kid, and I figured it was because he didn't spend as much time outside as I would have liked. By then the video games had started to set in. I limited the use at my house, and refused to buy them for them, but there were no rules at dad's house, and he would spoil them rotten!

As the kids became adults, they would see the truth as it is. Ryan asked to see the divorce files when he turned eighteen, because he wanted to know the truth. I showed him the file drawer with all the paperwork, for the court cases every time I had to take their father back to court. He refused to pay for half of Ricky's braces, even though he made ten times what I made, and I had to take him back to court. Of course, he waited until the poor kid was in the chair and then called the dentist office to say he wasn't paying! He refused to pay for half of Robbie's computer for school, required for his IEP plan, so we went back to court. He wrote bad checks that were a month late when he was paying child support, back to court. He refused to take the kids for his regularly scheduled visits, again back to court! They stay in touch with their father as they are all grown up, but from a safe distance. He's a very sick person in many ways, both physically and emotionally, but he is the only father they have.

MY SECOND HUSBAND

I met my second husband about a year after my first husband and I separated his name is Bill. I technically met him through a matchmaker, but he didn't want people to know that. I was really the first person he was with after his marriage of twenty-five years. We connected immediately, and I thought he was a good solid family man. In reality, that was from the outside looking in. From the inside, his family was very dysfunctional, and extremely controlling. He worked in the "family" business that he started with his father, and although he was forty years old when I met him, he still had to answer to them for everything he did. He lied to me, and wasn't actually divorced when I met him. I found the paperwork that he had started it, hidden in his kitchen after we had been dating for about six months. He was quite the introvert, and as much as I learned from him, I taught him how to come out of his shell.

I was also looking at the time for a location to open a deli. He happened to own a strip mall, and had a vacancy. I made an offer to rent the place and open a deli, and he insisted that I had to buy the equipment inside, because he didn't want to dispose of it. Knowing that he had a soft serve machine that I could sell for twice the price, I agreed. I listed the ice cream machine and got three times what I paid for the whole place!

I wasn't looking for any special treatment as far as the business went, but as my boyfriend, I thought he might help a little bit! He did help hang some drywall for me, but when it came down to helping me fix a countertop the day before I opened, going to a parade was more important. I was doing a training with the employees, (which included his daughter), and showing them how to clean the meat slicer. I was so exhausted from doing all the last minute finish work, and trying to get the place open, while still raising three children, that my hand slipped, and I cut my index finger to the bone. I walked into the bathroom, sat down on the floor, and went into shock! Bill's office was right next door, and his daughter ran over to tell him I was hurt. I barely remember anything, other than him picking me up, putting me in his car, and taking me to the emergency room to sew my finger back on! At one point, I had fallen behind on my rent, and his father came in looking for payment. I told him I would discuss it with Bill, not him. He got very angry and said if I ever married him, he would never step foot in our home. Bill didn't marry me until after his father passed away. Strangely enough, his father comes to see me every so often from the other side, and always tells me how much he really liked me!

Bill was a really nice guy, although very damaged from the

marriage to his high school sweetheart and a very controlling family. He felt everyone wanted him for his money, and that was the farthest thing from my mind! He seemed like a solid family man, and I truly believed he wouldn't cheat on me. I almost wonder if that wasn't my motivation, although I truly did love him. Unfortunately it was a long time coming! We dated on and off for about nine years, never living together. As much as my kids loved him, he insisted he didn't want to live the family life any more. He rarely stayed a night at my house; it seemed I was always going to his. At one point he decided to have a vasectomy without even discussing it with me. I would have wanted another child, being only thirty at the time. He asked me to take him to the appointment, and then referred to me as "his driver!" I was pretty upset, to say the least. His sister came over to visit while he was recovering, and he asked me to stay out of sight, since after about six months we still hadn't met. I had the opportunity to go to Venice that first year with a few friends. Bill said he couldn't go, because his family would never allow him to shut the business down for a week. He told me when I came back, that he didn't think he was going to hear from me again.

At one point in time, I got the feeling he was cheating on me, and still dating girls from the matchmaker, even though he told me no. I got up in the morning after staying at his place, and called the locksmith whose name was on his safe. I said I was his wife, and needed to get into the safe, but couldn't figure out how to open it. (I copied the code down when he had left it on the bathroom counter). The locksmith walked me through getting it open. Just as I did, and had all the names and numbers of the girls he had received in my hand, he decided not to go to work because of the weather, and walked into the bedroom. I was sitting there on the floor stark naked, trying to explain why I just broke into his safe! It was clear I wasn't interested in the money, there were thousands sitting on the shelves. It was also hard to take the high ground on the girls when I was clearly in the wrong! It did become a running joke through the years though, if I couldn't get the safe open it was because I had clothes on!

I came to realize too late, that he and his family had a philosophy; if you weren't blood related, you had no value. He also had no friends, because he was raised being told that friends only want something from you. He never learned that it's a give and take. If he had friends, they might have given him some pointers in the marriage! Sadly, as far as he and his family were concerned, even his wife of twenty-five years was worthless. His children were brought up with the same mentality, so they didn't respect their mother, and talked about the son's wife behind her back, as well as his aunt by marriage and I'm most certain me.

His children even refused to interact with my children, and refused to recognize them as family. I on the other hand, had to employ his daughter in all of the different businesses I owned. He hoped I could instill some kind of value system in her that he and his wife had failed to do. At one point, she tried to put me out of business after working for me at the Day Spa. After being there for about six weeks, she tried to undermine me every chance she got with the staff. When she ended up embroiled in a lawsuit I had against an esthetician she was in cahoots with, she threatened suicide, and was institutionalized. I ended up dropping the lawsuit to save my marriage, but not before spending ten thousand dollars on lawyers, and having her cost me a hundred thousand dollars of lost business!

His family was so rude to me, that I got to the point that I would rather stay home then subject myself to their negativity. My step son even had the nerve to tell his father not to bring me to his son's baptism! It was the first time Bill finally stood up for me and said if I wasn't welcome he wouldn't be there, either. He still had less of a backbone when it came to his daughter. Whatever she demanded, she got. He had no boundaries with his own children, which created huge problems down the road. His children were spoiled, arrogant, rude and narcissistic. They disliked me from the get go, because I stood between daddy and the wallet a lot. I would point out that it wasn't appropriate to put your sixteen-year-old-daughter's name on a joint checking account like you were married, and tell her what's your is hers. I proved my point when she had a drunken party at the condo they lived in and got arrested when she was arguing with the police that she owned the condo and could do whatever she wanted to there. She got arrested for underage drinking! After we opened the day spa, she demanded that he let her borrow twenty thousand dollars to buy a house and convert it into a day spa for her. She started yelling at me saying he should have built it for her, because I was nobody, and she was his daughter. I let him know, it would be the end of the marriage if he gave her the money. Instead, she decided to tell the city where she put the offer on the house that she was going to do it with or without permits. They made it clear she would never get a license in their town. She finally decided to give up, politics were not her *forte*! I also found out he had her on the payroll for his business. He had been hiding it from me for years. She lived in our apartment house rent free, and had income from a roommate, she worked at her own nail salon part-time when she felt like it, and was flying to Mexico for a while having an affair with a guy she met on vacation. He bought her a car and paid for her gas. He was able to fund all that, and not put into the marriage financially.

We finally split up after the nine years of dating, because it seemed obvious to me he was never going to marry me or move the relationship forward. After a few months of separation, he came back and asked me to marry him. He sent me six dozen roses, and I said yes. We set a wedding date of February 7, 2002, it was my youngest son Ryan's birthday. We didn't tell anyone we were getting married, because he didn't want to tell his kids. He knew they wouldn't approve. I didn't know his mother knew, and in fact years later he told me he married me because she told him he should! The day we got married in Las Vegas, my oldest son fell and broke his elbow, trying to throw a snowball with a golf ball in it at his younger brother. I was on the phone back and forth with his father during the surgery. When we came back and told the kids, my youngest son Ryan got all upset and started to cry. I asked him what was wrong, because he loved Bill like he was his dad. He said “I know, but now you’ll have another kid and I won’t be the baby anymore!” He was ten years old already, and only his dad truly treated him like the baby of the family. I assured him, we weren’t having any more children!

Bill moved in, but only partially and still couldn’t fully commit to the relationship. He brought some clothes, but kept his apartment set up just in case, and slept at my house every day. Just because he married me, he clearly hadn’t committed one hundred percent to the marriage. I felt like I had made a mistake. I was very unhappy, and he refused to discuss it. This was a constant problem with him; he would talk to his kids instead of me whenever he had a problem. He did it again, he told his son he wanted an annulment, and had him get the paperwork. I was so pissed when he showed me; I just signed the paperwork and said good-bye. He went back to his apartment, and we went our separate ways. It didn’t last long, though. We ran into each other nine months later, at a wedding we both ended up at. By seeing each other, we realized how much we still cared about each other, and immediately started talking and dating. We decided to get remarried again before the end of the year, that way he received the financial benefit of an offset I had to his capital gains, since he sold his strip mall. He told me he had been in counseling since we split up, and he really seemed like a changed man. The first year of our marriage was amazing!

Years later, when he wanted to hurt me, he would say he married me for the money, but I know he loved me as much as I loved him. We just weren't very compatible people. He wasn't communicative, very stubborn, and he didn't enjoy sex. All he wanted to do was work, save his money, and spend any down time with his family, not me. The only reason we stayed together as long as we did, was because he enjoyed traveling with me. I'm a person that really enjoys sex, and needs intimacy. He would have no problem going for six months without any physical contact. He was never the initiator. He did get a little bit better as the years went by, but he was also very cheap. I worked as hard and as many hours as he did, and I was the person paying for everything. Even if we went out for dinner! He would bank everything he made and say it was for our future. In the end, I lost everything I worked twenty years for, and he put all of his assets in his mother's name to hide them, and we were divorced. I've seen him a few times since; he still seems miserable, and upset that I love my life without him. My middle son sees him on occasion, although not very often or regularly. He was closer to Bill than his own father, and it was difficult on him to see us divorce.

Before We Married

During the time that I was dating Bill, I was always very self-sufficient. It was a struggle financially, however, since the child support was sporadic. He refused to help me financially in any way, and had to answer to his parents for everything he did, even though he was forty years old! The deli wasn't very profitable, it was still being established, so I ended up taking a job as a cocktail waitress at a strip club, that my lovely ex-husband arranged. He used to frequent those places when we were married, telling me it was a breakfast meeting with the guys, for "legs and eggs!" The place was a real den of iniquity! I only lasted about three weeks there, because I was apparently cutting into the money the other girls were making. I was there to work and make as much money as I could. It was also a cash bar, so I would pay for a tray of beer, and stand at the door with it when the bachelor parties would roll in by the busload. I hustled, and I would make about five hundred dollars for a night. Since my deli was slow in taking off, it was paying my mortgage.

One Friday night I forgot to bring my dinner, and asked Bill if he could bring it down for me. He brought it, but refused to come into the building. It was OK for me to work there, but he wouldn't step one foot into a place like that! The truth is, after witnessing some of the disgusting sex acts happening right out in the open with people I knew, (these were married friends, I knew their wives and families), if I'd stayed any longer, I probably never would have let a man touch me again! Most of the strippers were on drugs, and I even ran into my old babysitter that had run away from home working there. I was never so happy to be fired in my life!

The deli only made so much money a week; it was still being established, and it was the wrong type of food for the area. Although I was written up in some major magazines, the people with money didn't frequent often enough. A lot of the politicians from Rhode Island would come down for lunch, but only about once a month. I was also working way too many hours again, and I had to keep the kids with me there. I put the business up for sale and recovered all of my investment plus. The people that bought it however, changed the entire menu, lost all of the clientele, and went out of business in less than ninety days.

Bill then ended up helping me renovate a pizza truck that he had found in the woods, and I opened a hot dog and sandwich stand in the parking lot of my father's donut shop. I worked there for the summer, mother's hours, and really wasn't pulling ahead when I had to pay for daycare as well. It would have been a good part time income, but not enough to take care of a family. I tried putting my younger sister Shirley to work there just to keep her busy while I was opening my daycare, but she kept shutting off the breakers instead of the lights, and everything kept spoiling! I decided to sell it, and again, made about twice what the unit cost me. My angels have always made sure that I made money on houses and most of my businesses, and have had enough money to support myself and my children.

While I was there, however, I had yet another run-in with my brother William. He came over to the hot dog stand, and started engaging me in conversation. He was telling me how he had lost his job as a machinist, and wanted to know if my ex-husband might be able to get him a job in the union. I've never been one to hold a grudge against anyone, and I figured maybe he wasn't drinking and was trying to change. He went into my father's office and I continued working. A short time later, I decided to go into my father's office to say goodbye for the day, and as soon as I opened the door from the outside, my brother William jumped on top of me from the top of the stairs inside the building, and tried to bite the nose off of my face! I screamed, he got off, and I called the police. I had deep marks on either side of my nose, as well as cuts and abrasions from being jumped on and thrown to the ground. He was arrested for assault, and I got a restraining order on him. My father's response was the standard answer; "I guess he didn't mean to do it, because you still have a nose!"

MY DAYCARE BUSINESSES

I was having a very difficult time finding a decent daycare for my youngest son after I separated from my first husband. I would pick him up with diapers that were not changed, and the kids were covered in food and dirt from not being watched. It was difficult to work having him with me in a playpen at the deli as well. I decided to open a daycare center. All of my life I've had a knowing if I was supposed to do something. I have always blindly trusted that knowing. I had ten thousand dollars in my pocket from working nights and selling the deli and the hot dog stand.

I found a great building to rent and took an option to buy it within one year. The best business advice my father ever gave me, was to never open a business unless you can buy the building. That way if you're successful, they can't throw you out, and steal your business idea! Realistically, he always thought the worst of people. But was he said was a good idea because you're investing your money into the property, instead of paying the mortgage for someone else.

I really had the angels on my side opening this business. I had no clue how expensive it was going to be! I bought the contents of the building again, it had been a sporting goods store, and sold them at a profit. I had to re-do the septic system and try to divide up the interior of the building. Everyone I hired was wonderful, and I ended up paying them over time. I ended up going bankrupt after the first divorce, because I was left with a ton of bills from the marriage and very little income. I was truly blessed to be able to buy the building after the first year, being a woman, with a bankruptcy, and a prayer.

I started the first summer at the daycare with five children enrolled, three of them mine. For licensing purposes, I had to hire enough teachers and staff to get the license for a hundred and twenty-five children because of the size of the building, and then lay them all off! I also had to get my teaching certificate in Massachusetts, so I got my degree doing the courses online at night while my kids were sleeping. I just kept praying, and knowing I was supposed to do what I was doing, and by September I had seventy-five children enrolled. I had zero help from Bill at the time, even though we were still dating. It seemed I always did the best and got the farthest when I was by myself.

There are no easy businesses. I worked at least sixty hours a week when I opened it, but I made sure to close for the weekends so I could have some balance in my life, and time with my children. The children in the daycare, for the most part, were wonderful, but many of the parents left a lot to be desired. I had a very wealthy set of parents that had two little girls enrolled, ages four and five. They continually sent them in to school with sour smelly hair from going to bed with a baby bottle full of milk. They also weren't toilet trained at that age. When talking with the father about the problem, he likened them to dogs; "When they're ready they'll just do it!" After they kept bringing them with moldy food and dirty clothes, and not caring about what we were telling them at the daycare, I finally decided to file a 51A abuse and neglect complaint with the state. As childcare workers, we were mandated reporters. The father was notified first, and came marching into my building very angry! On his way to my office, he told the staff to call the police because he planned on killing me! I heard him coming and called 911. Fortunately, the police arrived quickly!

I also had a parent who refused to pay her copay for her state funding, and accused a female teacher of molesting her three year old daughter in the bathroom! Again, with the camera footage, you could see that the teacher couldn't fit into the tiny one stall bathroom, and her entire body was in the hallway at all times. The mother pushed it all the way to court, having the little girl go through an exam with a doctor and all. They wanted me to suspend the teacher until it went to court, some nine months after the complaint. Had I done that, it would have destroyed her reputation. Not only did the Judge drop all the charges, she ordered the mother to undergo psychiatric counseling! All this because she didn't want to pay the money she owed!

That daycare operated for ten years, in Massachusetts, until the economy and the competition changed. I opened a second daycare in the next state, Rhode Island, only fifteen minutes away, after about five years. The second one actually did better than the first, because the licensing requirements were different. Timewise, it overlapped the other facility for a little over ten years as well. I ran two of the only NAYEC accredited daycares in the area. They were both very high quality and run by the book. I was never one to not speak my mind however, and I had a competitor that took it to heart!

There was a chain of daycares in the area that were not very good quality. In fact they were dirty, dangerous, and operating without following the licensing requirements. The owner was an elected politician in Rhode Island. She had opened a few of her chain daycares in Massachusetts, and was shut down and banned from the state due to the sheer number of violations and children's injuries. I actually had parents bring them to my daycare believing that their children may have been molested there as well, but didn't want to open a can of worms! When I asked a licensor in Rhode Island why she was being allowed to operate in the state, I was told that she was so large, that if they shut her down, they would have no place to "warehouse" the children! I told her I didn't realize we were in the business of "warehousing" children! I'm sure the comments I had to make about the children that I was getting in my centers after being injured in hers got back to her. She tried to put me out of business!

The Frame-Up

I had a full-time director running each of the facilities. The Massachusetts director had been with me almost since opening. The Rhode Island director was a fairly new, probably about three months on the job. She had just found out she was pregnant, and had no loyalty to me. (Her husband was apparently not the father.) She hired a new office assistant a few days prior to me leaving for a ten-day vacation. While I was gone, the new assistant had been offering all the employees a job at the competing center, including the director, and stealing large quantities of my supplies and educational materials. The day I came back, I apparently caught everyone by surprise. Since I have cameras in the facility, I had everything on film, which I have saved until today. When I came in to my office, the new assistant got up from her desk, and walked into one of the classrooms. She spoke briefly with the teacher, and then picked up a pile of supplies and headed to the front door with it. She left it in the hallway, and then came back into the office. A moment later, the teacher she was speaking with brought a crying child into the office and sat her in a chair next to the director. The girl was kicking her feet on the chair, so the director placed her on the floor so she didn't injure her legs. Then the new assistant starts packing up more things from her desk, stands up and announces that she quits! I was shocked. I had just walked in the door! I asked why, what was going on, what happened? She said she didn't like the way I ran my daycare center. (The director was sitting there with her head down, and said nothing.) I asked her what she was talking about, she'd only been there for two weeks, and I've been gone most of that time. She said nothing more, walked into the classroom again, whispered to the teacher, picked up the supplies she placed in the hallway, and walked out the door! I watched her on camera pull out of the parking lot, and into the business across the street. Within a few minutes, the police arrived, along with a Department of Children, Youth and Families social worker. (DCYF) They stated that they received a phone call saying I had thrown a little girl across my office, and I had also withheld food from her while I was threatening her! (Withholding food is a separate, serious violation.) Not only did I not speak to the little girl, I didn't touch her, and her teacher came back to get her at lunchtime. They were on an agenda! An allegation of abuse had been made, and I needed to stay away from my business until I had a formal hearing with the DCYF. In the meantime, I got nowhere trying to file a police report on all the stolen items, or getting anyone to actually look at the camera footage. Even the state police wouldn't get involved when they heard who the other daycare operator was. I ended up having to hire an expensive attorney, who at the time had more political pull than she did. He talked to DCYF, and told them if they didn't watch the camera footage, he would get a judge involved and have an injunction issued against them. In the meantime, the teacher that was in cahoots with her and that that was offered a new job at her center, was telling all the parents that I had abused a child, and that they should take their children to other centers. Of course, the director there gave her notice almost as quickly. I moved my director from the Massachusetts center there, and I took over for her. She got the place under control, and actually had the parents that knew there was no truth to the story write letters on my behalf. This included the mother of the child I was accused of abusing. The lawyer got the issue dismissed, but not before telling me that DCYF was told to drag it out as long as possible, to cost me as much as possible so I would go out of business! A week later, I received a written offer in the mail from the politician, offering to buy my center for a ridiculous amount of money! Although she lost her bid for re-election, and her centers were eventually closed for violations, she reopened under her son's name with a new scam for the state. She now employs her own staff psychiatrist and labels the children in her centers as ADD or learning disabled, so she can receive extra state funding. It's hard to believe this stuff really happens in life, but it does! I do believe that everyone gets their due karma somehow. She should be very concerned!

The Rhode Island parents didn't like to pay their bills any more than the Massachusetts parents. I would spend every Thursday in court trying to collect on bad checks and balances they would leave on their accounts. We would have to take the children into the center while they were pending with the state, waiting for an approved voucher. Many times, the parents didn't submit the paperwork in a timely manner, or would have higher co-pays than they originally thought. In those cases, the parent would just remove the children and go to another daycare. I was left holding the bag on thousands that I had no choice but to try and collect in court. I was approached on more than one occasion by attorneys asking my advice on the procedures, since they didn't spend a lot of time there, and many of them thought I was an attorney!

As soon as I opened the Massachusetts center, I also started a non-profit community partnership program for four of the towns in Massachusetts. This was the vehicle that the state used to fund low income children at the time. When it became a political game, I resigned my position. It was, however, quite the accomplishment. No one had been able to get the people to the table, or get it funded, although many people before me had tried. All of my grants that I wrote were fully funded every year, and it still operates today in the towns of Swansea, Seekonk, Dighton and Rehoboth Massachusetts. With the changing times however, the focus for it has changed from group daycare centers to home daycares.

CHANGING WITH THE TIMES!

When the economy changed in Massachusetts, and I decided it was about time to do something different with the building, I opened a children's hair salon in half of the day care building. I had trained privately in the cosmetology field, long before I think I was legally old enough! My hairdresser when I was young was an instructor for one of the schools in Rhode Island. She privately trained me and groomed me to buy her rental apartment building, which included her hair salon when I turned eighteen. Unfortunately, it never panned out. I broke up with my fiancé and didn't feel confident to take that responsibility on by myself. I had my cosmetology school diploma, but never actually got the license. I also hadn't done hair in years, and wasn't able to actually work in the business I was opening. That made it very difficult to run. I was at the mercy of trying to find hairdressers that held a class 1 license and wanted to cut children's hair. That was like finding a needle in a haystack! None of the stylists wanted to stay, and the parents would bring the children in with head-lice, or screaming at the top of their lungs! It was so difficult, that I decided to close not only the children's salon, but also the daycare, since most of the kids were being put into the public schools under a new initiative called Y2K. That program encompassed full-time preschool, full-time kindergarten, and before and after school programs. That would leave me with just infants, and you lose money on them due to the state ratios. My director that had been with me for ten years also gave me notice that she was leaving. I paid for her to receive her bachelor's degree while she worked for me. I kept her on salary and allowed her to change her hours to accommodate her education. Of course, she said she wouldn't leave after, but people always have to follow their own journey.

Bill and I got married around this time, and decided to take all the kids on a cruise, and then tackle the redesign of the building, and make it a very upscale full day spa. We knew it would be the last big vacation for a while. We took his mother with us since she was alone, and then his daughter, who was twenty-five at the time, took a fit that we didn't include her! We explained that she's an adult, and we didn't ask her for the same reason we didn't ask her brother and his family. She then went off the rails that we should take and pay for my three children who are all under eighteen and at home, and not pay for her. She wanted to go and said if we paid she would pay us back. Needless to say, she racked up a huge liquor bill, was never seen, and never paid us back! She also messed up the room arrangements that put my three boys on a different floor on the other end of the ship. This made it much more difficult for me to monitor them.

We had taken a prior cruise before we were married, and Bill allowed her to go and take her boyfriend with her at the time. They were both sixteen years old, and although Bill was in denial, they were clearly sleeping together and having sex under his roof. We ended up in Jamaica and paid a private cab to take us on a tour of the Island. At the end of the tour, although we had agreed on a price with the driver, he pulled a knife on us and demanded all of our money. I told Bill not to give it to him, there were three of us and one of him! He said he didn't want his daughter getting hurt and gave him what he had in his wallet. The rest of us claimed we had no money, and he was satisfied with what Bill had given him. For this reason, I will never set foot in Jamaica again! Although it's a beautiful country, the locals are literally "in your face" trying to harass and steal from you.

I tried to include Bill with the plans on the day spa as much as I could. He unfortunately wasn't overly interested, and preferred that I took care of it myself. I handled most of our business dealings, and finances, with the exception of one construction company. When we got married, I added him as a corporate officer on to all of my companies, and gave him half of my stock. He did not do the same for me. I think I was forever trying to get him to understand that I wanted him for him, not what he had. Sadly he never really got it until we divorced. There were many times that I was very overwhelmed handling all the finances and businesses in the marriage. I did all the books and accounting for my two daycares, his two construction companies, a real estate company that we owned together, and handled all the rentals and problems with the tenants we had in five rental units. I paid all the bills, and I was the only one worrying about the money, because my companies were paying for everything we owned. All this while I was trying to be a good mom, raise my own three children, and keep up the home! For the most part, other than a small stipend Bill would put into the house, the burden of all the finances fell on me and my companies, not his. That included any trips we would take, and we would travel three to four times a year. We also took his mother, my children and father, and ourselves, to my middle son's graduation from the Air Force Academy. I paid for everything except for his spending money! I even had to buy my father a new naval uniform with all new medals so he could pin my son at the graduation, and even he didn't offer to pay me back for the cost!

Another lesson that I've had to learn in life; receive and respond! I no longer offer anything financially unless it's been offered to me first! I'll always be ok, and have money, but that's because I know that my angels and God take care of me. No one is supposed to live in want. Money is not what's important. There's no money in heaven! You can't take it with you! Its sole purpose here is security, and to help people in need. Otherwise, to hoard it is just misguided!

Sometimes it takes people a long time to realize, money does not make you happy. Just as many wealthy people commit suicide as people without money. There's no need for money on the other side!

THE DAY SPA

We got the day spa open in 2007. I used the services of a spa consultant, since it wasn't really my background, and I wanted it to be done properly. Unfortunately, she used a model for a medical-spa, rather than the model that most spas in the area operated under. This put a huge financial burden on the business, because employees were getting paid even if they had no clientele. Most places pay strictly on a commission basis. My employees were making minimum wage plus a commission on services and retail, plus gratuity. The bottom line was that they were making the majority of the money, not the spa. The first year we did wonderful, because the economy was booming, and there was nothing like it in the area. Then the floor fell out, and the economy crashed! I have no idea how I survived as long as I did. I was able to keep the doors open for ten years, and keep the revenue basis close to the same, even though the cost of supplies, utilities, wages, taxes, and insurance continued to rise. The other businesses were supporting it for the last few years it operated. I also had invested steadily into the stock market over a twenty-year period, and when things got bad, I used all the money I had made.

We opened it under the premise that I wouldn't have to actually work in the business, which in reality, I don't believe ever works in any business. It's the old story of while the cat's away the mice will play! I had people stealing so much that other employees couldn't do their job because someone stole the items they needed to use! The employees still didn't want to say anything though. One girl walked out with all the supplies to do the acrylic nails, and the only reason I found out, was because the nail tech overheard her saying she was taking the drill next, which would leave her with no drill to use! Obviously the police were called, and she returned what she stole, except she had damaged all the brushes and tools so much we still couldn't use them!

We hired a girl as the general manager, on the recommendation of the consultant, who came from a large upscale spa called the Canyon Ranch. Part of her salary and benefit package, included an apartment to live in. When not enough revenue was coming in, and she was refunding multiple customers for complaints, I decided to start watching her comings and goings on the camera. She was required to work a 45 hour work week, including Saturdays. The staff started coming to me, and telling me they had no products to do the services with. I didn't understand how this was happening, since she had the authority to order whatever we needed. I then found out from the staff that they were told to NOT speak with me, and she told them they would be reprimanded if they did. She told them I didn't want to be bothered by them, and made me out to be a horrible person to the staff. She then started berating me, saying I was mean to my employees and I should just let her run it the way she wanted to run it. Meanwhile, I saw that she showed up to work in a jogging suit and stayed about fifteen minutes before leaving, sometimes returning for the day and sometimes not. She was actually only putting in about fifteen or twenty hours per week, and had no idea what was going on in the business. Apparently, she had married someone she didn't love, and had been having an affair on my time! It was quite the process to terminate her, because not only was she under contract, but it now included an eviction! As it is now in society, she took to the internet to slander me, and claim I was a horrible boss, and it was entirely my fault that the business wasn't operating properly. She finally was gone, and regressed in life big time, moving back in to her mother's house, and took a job somewhere as a receptionist She used to tell me how difficult it was to function in a society where no one was as intelligent as she was! She did eventually divorce and remarry. I'm not sure if it was with the guy she was cheating with!

After that fiasco, I ended up having to step in as the general manager myself, on top of the rest of my responsibilities and businesses and learn the computer and booking system. As time went on, not only was I running the facility, but filling in as the receptionist, and doing services when we were short staffed. Of course, once someone has the owner, they then kept requesting me, and I ended up working in the business approximately fifty or sixty hours per week, doing nails, aesthetic services, and covering the front desk. It helped on the income end, because I wasn't paying the technicians, but some of them got upset acting like it was taking clients from them. It was a difficult business to operate, there's just way too much drama. Everyone in the beauty industry thinks they are the best of the best! Interestingly many of them couldn't even figure out their paycheck! Being a high-end facility, many of the guests that came in weren't very nice either. They wanted to be catered to like they were the best thing since popcorn! Then you have the ones that are just scam artists and complain about everything so they can get a refund! It seemed like there were a lot of days that you couldn't make anyone happy!

I had a young man come in and apply for a cook's position about a year after firing the general manager. We had a café at the time inside of the spa. Unfortunately, it didn't do enough business, because people never thought to go there outside of the spa patrons. He had piercings and tattoos all over his body, but there was something about his way, that I took to immediately. His name was Tom, a young Portuguese man about the age of twenty-eight. I explained that he would have to change his look, remove the piercings, hide the tattoos, and he agreed. Tom worked his way from the kitchen to the desk, and then became the guest services manager. Then I helped him go back to school for hairdressing, which was his passion. He eventually ended up being my hair salon manager, but never built up enough confidence to actually act as a manager. He was always afraid of people not liking him. He wasn't comfortable reprimanding or firing people, but became a go-between for the staff. He was an absolute godsend to me! He became my right arm in the business, and was with me for eight years. I think it broke both of our hearts for him to finally make the decision to move on in his career. He was more like a son to me than an employee. His path was different however, and he went on to rent a chair in another facility. Many of the clients followed him however, as they usually do in these situations, and again the business took a big financial hit. The hair salon never really took off, because most stylists don't want to work in such a controlled environment. Being upscale, they were required to wear uniforms, do laundry, clean, and they weren't allowed to wear jeans, talk on the phone, play loud music, or chew gum. For these reasons, many of the stylists wouldn't stay long, and the clients didn't like the change, so they would go somewhere else or follow the technician.

CLOSING THE RHODE ISLAND DAYCARE

I closed the second daycare located in Rhode Island, in 2014, after my current director decided it was time to get married and move on. The number of children had dropped from seventy-five to twelve, because in that state most childcare is paid through state vouchers. When the economy nosedived, no one had money to pay privately, and if you weren't working you didn't get a voucher. I operated averaging twelve children for almost two years, hoping the economy was going to recover. I decided that not only did I not have the time to sit in the daycare and be the director for forty hours a week, but I also didn't have the desire, when it was only holding its own. The children and staff were wonderful there, but most of the parents were horrible. If they could have tossed the kids to you while they were driving by, I truly believe many of the parents would have. They clearly weren't connected or caring to the children they had, and it was heart breaking to see. Not all the parents were like this, but the majority were. I was constantly having arguments with parents about paying their copays and bringing supplies like diapers for their children. I decided to close, and opened a resale shop, so that the building wasn't empty and open to being vandalized. I had the building and the business for sale for over five years, and since the economy was terrible, I never could get anyone interested in buying it. But I kept it on the market while I opened and operated the resale shop.

* * *

The Consignment Store

My youngest brother, Albert, who had been working with my father in the business his entire life, was given the job of cleaning out the "hoarder house" we grew up in, because the Board of Health and the Building Department in the town wanted it torn down. It was collapsing from not being maintained for years. Quite the eyesore for the neighbors! The roof had caved in on part of the house, the bushes and yard had almost overgrown the house in the front and back and there was a hornet nest that was so large, you could hear the buzzing from across the street! The mailman was afraid to walk by because the quantity of bees going in and out was like a National Geographic movie! My brother had to call the exterminator in before he could even think about working on emptying the house. As much as my father would always spend top dollar for the best of everything, he never maintained anything he owned. If not for my brother, his business probably would have fallen down around him years ago!

When we were kids, my mother used to take us to the town dump. Instead of throwing trash away, she would pick through and bring it all home. The stuff was floor to ceiling in most rooms, it covered all the furniture, and there was a small path to walk on from room to room. Believe it or not, she had a good eye for value! Many of the items she brought home, other than all the clothing, were valuable antiques. As time went on, they became rarer and more valuable. Sadly, with the weather getting at it, most of it was moldy and rotted. My brother had the task of going through it all, and separating the garbage into a dumpster, and anything he thought was salvageable into a trailer truck for storage. He filled four tractor trailers with bins full of china, dishes, glassware, clothing, books, and more! I have no idea how many dumpsters he filled.

I decided to open the consignment shop at my father's bequest, to try and clean and sell some of the items. I ended up basically paying employees to clean and sell the items, but barely made enough to cover the electricity and other expenses. Again, between the staff and the public stealing everything, it was more work than it was worth. I still had the building up for sale, but was unable to sell, and figured I needed to put something in there that would generate some income.

I was now three years into the divorce from Bill, and I was left having to pay the bills for the majority of what we owned. I took a loan out on a duplex that I've owned for twenty-five years and decided to re-do the building in Pawtucket and turn it into a sports bar. The building was in really bad shape when I started the renovation, and I had to put much more into it than I originally planned. I had put a thirty-thousand-dollar roof on it when I had the daycare, and it was the only thing that didn't have to be replaced! Even though the money was going into improving a marital asset, I was considered in contempt of court because of the divorce order. I was able to run my businesses as usual, but not able to take the loan against the property. It's amazing how someone you can spend twenty years of your life with can be so horrible to someone they claimed to love because of money.

I was always very nice to my ex-husbands, during and after the divorces. I allowed my first husband to come to my home with his girlfriend of the week and his whole family, for every holiday or event that concerned the kids, until they all turned eighteen. I was never mean to my second husband, even though he ended up stealing all the money we had accumulated together. (He liked to save money in cash, and although I could have cleaned it all out, I didn't touch it, he took it all!) Everyone has to look in the mirror every day and be happy with the person they see. I know I am. I don't think either of them can say they are.

THE SPORTS BAR

While I was renovating the building, I was acting as the general contractor. I hired someone I went to high school with to do most of the renovations. The building consisted of two mobile trailers that were bolted together in the basement, around a slab on grade section that was the original building. The building was originally a real estate office in the 1950's. No one really remembered this, but we found the windows still intact inside the walls, with Alexion's Real Estate still lettered on them. Everyone did, however, remember the building being a famous restaurant in the 1970's and 1980's. It was called Allexion's Family Restaurant.

When I originally bought the building, around 2006, it had been a sports bar called Wetherlaine's. Mr. Wetherlaine was going through a divorce, and wanted to sell this location, and keep his other location in Attleboro. I rented the building with an option to buy when I put the daycare in it. The building was a mess then, and I had to constantly call him about roof leaks. It was so bad one day, I had to close the center and send all the kids home, as the rain was just pouring in. He told me to get it patched by someone myself and take it out of the rent. This is exactly what I did. He then took me to court to try and evict me from the property for non-payment of rent. When the case got in front of the judge, it was obvious that Wetherlaine was trying to sell it for more money to someone else since I had improved the property to start the daycare business, and he lost his case. I did go talk to the Alexion family at the time, since they were holding his mortgage, just in case he was in arears. If he had been, I could have just asked them to foreclose on him. Mr. Alexion had passed, and I spoke with his widow. She was a lovely woman. Their son also stopped in to see me; he was a fireman in Pawtucket until his retirement.

The renovation was a lot of work, with a lot of problems. I ended up hiring a friend's son to do the electrical work, who had absolutely no idea of the commercial code. I say friend with my tongue in my cheek. I had known Steve since I was a teenager, and was with my first boyfriend, Tony. Steve and his wife used to vacation with Tony and I in the summertime. Steve was a police officer in Pawtucket until retiring. He was the first person I ended up dating after Bill and I split up. Unbeknown to me, he was still living with his girlfriend, who he told me was in the process of moving out. I then saw an engagement picture pop up one night on my Facebook page of the two of them. She clearly had no idea he was cheating on her, and I believed she was out of the picture. He tried explaining it away, like it was an arranged marriage or something, and pre-planned prior to meeting me! Needless to say, I was done with him, and later on down the road she was as well. I'm sure she must have caught wind, since I know I probably wasn't the only person he was cheating on her with.

Meanwhile, his son was ripping me off charging me time and materials. I spoke to him about it the first time I caught him, and he tried to make light of it and adjust the bill. I then had the other contractors watching his time, and he threatened to beat the crap out of them when he found out. I fired him, and then discovered he had installed all the wiring back to the breaker boxes wrong, and overloaded the new boxes he had installed It all had to be redone after being rejected by the electrical inspector. But his best screw-up, was installing all of the cable lines backwards for the twenty-something television sets that were going to go into the sports bar. Cable lines over a certain number of feet are directional. He knew this, but he had no clue which direction to install them! I was originally going to sue him for the damage and over thirty-thousand dollars of extra work he required on the job, and my lawyer sent him a letter to put him and his insurance company on notice. His father, having the largest ego I've ever seen, accused me of making it up because I was upset about him lying and cheating on me. I never pursued the lawsuit, only because it would be again thousands of dollars to the lawyer, and years of extra stress for me. I know that everyone gets in life what they put out. Enough said.

While we were under construction, everyone was hearing noises and catching things out of the corner of their eye. I always knew the building was haunted, but never knew by whom. When they were opening up the wall to install a large ventilation system, they found a brown paper grocery bag full of clothing in the ceiling. Then they started pulling out a sneaker, a wallet, a pair of pants, mail, magazines, and medication bottles. Everyone fully expected there to be a body up there! Apparently, there was a cook who would sleep in the storage area when it was a restaurant, and he would shove his belongings above him in the ceiling to hide them. His name was Fred.

After the Sports Bar was open, employees would see him walk through the dining room and disappear. I would come in every morning and find lights on, and hear him rattle all the dishes next to me to get my attention. I thought for sure the cooks were leaving the lights and the hood fans on when they left at night, but they insisted they weren't! I ended up watching the cameras, and they were right. They turned everything off when they left, and about two or three in the morning, the hood fans and lights would go on, as would the overhead fluorescents!

I tried to move Fred into the light, but he wanted to stay where he was. He told me he had a drinking problem when he was alive, and also had a mental disorder. He was on medication for it, which was what we found. He said he fell in the street, and died hitting his head against the curb. He went back to the restaurant because to him it was his home. He enjoyed his job, and the Alexion's were always very kind to him. We ended up coming to an agreement. If there was a problem in the building, he can turn on the lights to get my attention; otherwise, they needed to stay off, since they were costing me an arm and a leg! He understood and was grateful that I was alright with him staying. Every time I came in and found the lights on after that, there was a problem! Once it was a refrigerator door left open, another time it was a refrigerator failure. Another time I really had to look to find the problem, but I knew there was one, or he wouldn't have turned on the lights. It ended up that the plug had been pulled out of the wall that powered half of the kitchen. I'm sure he's still there, probably a little sadder since he can't cook and play in the kitchen any more, as it has been turned into an African market.

The bar came out amazing and added another thirty or so hours a week to my already busy work schedule! Fortunately I rented a house to live in that was between the spa and the bar, so I would go back and forth, and it wouldn't take long to get home at night. Many a night I would have to work at the bar until we closed at one in the morning. You never knew if it was going to be crazy busy or not. I would book bands to have live music, starting out seven days a week, and dwindling down to three nights a week. Everything costs money, and everyone thinks if you're in business you're rich. I have no idea how much the business really brought in, because bartenders seem to be the best at playing the register and stealing the money. They ring one sale and leave the ticket open, pocketing everything that's not food. I remember them going through four bottles of Raspberry Stoli one week, and only one drink was rung into the register. The manager at the time told me they were out and I needed to order more, and I asked him what happened to the four that came in last week. He then said we must not have received it, although he signed for the delivery. After, I showed him that it wasn't being rung through the register, and the empty bottles were sitting out next to the dumpster.

The managers were just as bad as the bartenders. I have had two of them arrested and charged with the theft of over fifteen hundred dollars each. The vodka was the last straw for me, however. If you can't be there all day and night to make sure they aren't stealing the liquor and the money, or the bar isn't doing a ridiculous volume to make up for the theft, it's not worth keeping open. I closed it one month prior to having to close the day spa, hoping I could still sell it and save the rest!

HOW I OPENED UP AS A MEDIUM

About a year after Bill moved out I was on a dating site, and met was my Twin Flame, Rob. Twin flame is the name for a very specific type of relationship that very few people encounter in their lifetime. Supposedly, there are only 144,000 on earth at any given time. Even fewer end up together in this lifetime because of the intensity of the relationship, the fear associated with it, and whether or not you both awaken enough to learn how to make decisions that are heart centered, not from your ego or your brain. Prior to reincarnating, your soul splits into two, and comes back into two separate bodies. You get to experience much more that way, and it's usually a rocky road in life for both. But once you magnetize, and reconnect in this lifetime, if you become intimate you have soul recognition, and it sets you on a spiritual path and your life's true purpose. The night we actually met on the dating site, he had just found out that his father was in the hospital on life support, and being an only child, the decision to pull the plug and end his life fell on him. As anyone can imagine, this was a traumatic time in his life. He and his father had not been getting along, and he hadn't seen him in sometime prior to finding out he was in the hospital.

I was honored to be able to go through the ordeal with him, as much as I possibly could, since I had not yet met him in person. The following week, after the funeral, I invited him over to my house for a home cooked meal. I figured it had probably been a while since he'd had one. One thing led to another, and he ended up spending the night. That's when something happened. When we got physical together, we had what's called a Kundalini awakening. I had no idea at the time what it was, all I knew was that I left my body, similar to the day I died, and was literally having an out-of-body soul experience. It's also known as soul recognition, when two halves of the souls find each other. Obviously, something happened for him as well, because it started him running in fear. This is one of the results. The next result is your life starting to fall apart, so it can somehow fall together again. We saw each other a few more times over the next couple of months, but there were many extenuating circumstances with both of us. He was losing his home to foreclosure, and my sister Millie was dying of stage five cancer in California. He had difficulty with communication, and I was prone to jump to conclusions, out of my own fear of abandonment. We did keep in touch on and off for the next couple of years, but mainly from me "chasing", and him running. This is also a classic scenario with this type of relationship. After the first six months, I went to see a medium, because I couldn't get him out of my head, or my heart. I also didn't trust my own intuition. She recommended that I start meditating. This was not something I had ever tried before, although I had considered it. I always considered myself a very spiritual person, but never religious. She told me I should ask my guides to help open up my intuition when I was meditating. I guess at the time I didn't realize that my intuition and my psychic abilities were one in the same. As soon as I asked, it opened up like a floodgate! Be careful what you ask for! Apparently, they had just been waiting for me to ask to open back up! They started coming through like I hung up an open-for-business sign! I started having random people that I didn't know coming through at all hours of the day and night! It was actually frightening in some ways. It reminded me of my childhood!

I was working in my day spa business at the time doing aesthetic services, and putting my hands on the clients. Every person I touched brought a whole new flood of people and animals coming through! The first was a big white dog to jump in my lap! I asked the woman as discreetly as I could, that if I told her that I just saw a big white dog jump in my lap, would it mean anything to her? She got all excited, and said that she just put down her white Maltese the day before, and she was so happy to know that he was around. It continued from there. I asked her why she was so worried about her husband, and she proceeded to tell me he was alone in Florida right now. I started getting an image of a house in my head that I described to her. I thought it was the house she lived in, but the angle I was getting looked like it was on the water, and she said it didn't sound like her house. When she was getting ready to leave, she ran over to me with her cell phone, to show me a picture her husband just sent her of the house I had described, and the caption read, "our new house in Florida!" This continued with every person I got near. I was getting flooded with scenes of their life.

One woman I asked if she had been cleaning out an attic recently. She confirmed that her aunt had passed and they had cleaned out her attic the weekend prior. I told her I was seeing a sock monkey and wondered if she had found one. I thought the woman was going to pass out! She looked at me and said, "I found a sock monkey puppet in her attic."

The next woman, I described her entire living room for her, what the Christmas tree looked like, and where it was placed, what her daughter and husband looked like, what she had bought everyone for Christmas, and what her husband had gotten her and where he got it. She thought I had been in her house, and knew her husband and it was some kind of a joke. I thought she was kidding me, and just telling me yes to play along. That was it. I had definitely lost my mind! I needed to figure out how to make it stop. I started randomly calling every psychic and medium I could find listed online and asking for help.

I was very lucky to have been directed by the other side to teachers that helped me understand my abilities and how to turn them on and off. I ended up training for over a year, at places my mother who is also a medium, studied at over fifty years ago. My abilities grew very quickly, because I was apparently meant to do this work in this lifetime, and I've done it in many past lives. It took a while for me to come to terms with the abilities that I have been given, and understand that I have an important mission here on earth. Not only is the mission to learn and grow for my own soul, but it is also to help others heal the problems and heartache that they didn't heal with their loved ones before they passed to the other side.

As for Rob, my twin flame, we are not together as of the writing of this book. I know the angels want all twin flames to reunite, because the love they have when they're together is enough to help heal the world. It's also not a connection that can ever be severed. I feel what he feels and whether he knows it or not, he feels me as well. Everything happens in divine timing, and I will always have hope for his awakening, and our reuniting.

One of the most difficult things I have to go through, are the comments and remarks made by people who aren't yet awakened. I have never tried to push my belief system onto anyone, and would expect the same respect from anyone else. Having seen what I've seen however, and knowing what I know, it's difficult for me to deny that what I do is real. More real than the everyday motions we go through from day to day. There's absolutely no way I can deny that I'm conversing and seeing angels and souls from the other side, because there is absolutely no way I could know the things that I know otherwise. Like many people, I sometimes have a hard time believing it myself. I then remember that I have to trust. It's all about trusting that what I'm doing is God's work. God gave me this gift for a reason, and directs me every day to the people that need me, and the people that teach me more! There is a plan. We aren't necessarily meant to know what it is, because there would be no surprises in life, but there is a plan.

LOSING IT ALL

The sports bar came out wonderful, but again strapped me financially, it didn't take off as well as I had hoped, partly because it takes five years to establish a business, and partially due to not having a stable manager on site that was honest. I went through three managers, and all of them were stealing something. The first one wasn't showing up for her shifts, and was stealing time, as well as not managing the employees, and the next two stole a few thousand dollars of liquor and money out of the deposits. One was prosecuted; the other is still on the run with an arrest warrant issued. It's a tough business if you're not going to eat, sleep, and breathe it. I actually opened it hoping I could sell it, but with the divorce still tying everything up, that wasn't an option.

I now had another mortgage to cover, since I took the loan out against my residence. Bill wasn't held responsible by the courts to pay anything other than the mortgage on his three-family tenement that he was also living in. Because he was older than I was, he claimed he retired and collected social security. He also put the construction company he owned into his mother's name, to try and hide the assets, when he claimed he wanted to reconcile the marriage. If they followed him every day, they would see that he still went to work in his construction company every day like he always did. I was able to finally sell the house we lived in together, that I bought prior to the marriage, but it cost me ten thousand dollars to get out of it. He never had to pay any of the short falls. I had planned on refinancing both buildings that the businesses were in, but couldn't get a bank to touch it while I was in the middle of the divorce. They were concerned about the judge awarding the property differently than how they were titled. He knew if he strung me out long enough, I would end up running out of money, and he was right.

I settled the divorce with him, by agreeing to sell a piece of property I paid for, for half of what it cost. He insisted on buying twenty-six acres of land, to put his business on and relocate from Connecticut. He never looked into the zoning restrictions first however, and I trusted that he did his due diligence. I paid for the land, almost two hundred thousand dollars. (We both put fifteen thousand dollars apiece down to buy it.) He had an inside deal with an attorney to buy it for half that amount, and give me my own money back. I then was able to use the money to pay the back taxes and licenses to continue operating the businesses. I figured I'd still be fine, because I could then refinance once the divorce was over. Well, that still wasn't possible.

It's amazing how things happen and why. Apparently, when the bank originally wrote the mortgage, it was done improperly. They wrote a blanket mortgage for two properties, in two different states, as one SBA loan. The first thing they did wrong was requiring too many passive entities to guarantee the loan. I'm not sure what difference it made, but it's an SBA violation. They also never released the assets from the daycare that was in one of the buildings when it closed. There-fore, the construction costs could not be rolled into the new loan. The only way to fix it would be for the bank to split the loans, and remove the assets, making them conventional loans. Then I could refinance them again as SBA loans. The bank flatly refused. Their comments were that they were not the people that made the mistake at the bank, so they weren't about to fix it. The only option was to refinance with the SBA, and without their co-operation, it was off the table. No bank would touch it. There are lots of clauses in a mortgage that require the borrower to fix anything wrong with the mortgage paperwork, but apparently the bank is not required to do the same. Since they had attachments to the buildings and the contents, they weren't going to lose anything, and they didn't care. They offered to close the businesses, and hand over the deeds, or they would go after me legally, and it would just cost me more. I would still be foreclosed upon and out of the building and business in less than thirty days. I had no choice, Mother's Day was coming up, and I couldn't sell gift cards that I wouldn't be able to honor, so I closed everything with less than a week's notice.

I believe the employees could see the writing on the walls; I had been struggling financially for years, and killing myself physically working seven days a week, both night and day. In the end it was Gods will. I would never have been able to do the work I do if I still had even one of the businesses left. It was difficult to process at first, since everything I had worked for, for the last twenty-five years was gone, but the reality is, you can't take it with you. Money's only value is to take care of your needs, and to help those that need help. The angels make sure I have what I need to pay my bills, and in the end, that's all we really need.

People can be horrible however. You would think that with everything going on in the world, and the fact that businesses go out of business every day, I shouldn't be the nightly news. I was however. The news station went to the house I had been renting, and it just worked out that I had moved into my duplex the week prior. They claimed I packed up and moved in the middle of the night. Not likely, with the two truckloads of stuff I had, and the six guys working for the moving company to load it all. Then you have social media sites like Facebook and Google. Every employee I ever fired, including my mentally ill ex step daughter took to the internet to slander me, and make up all kind of stories. One woman even claimed I foreclosed on her house, like I was a bank. They wanted people to believe I opened just to sell gift cards and pocketed millions. They apparently don't know anything about business. Everything that came in financially went to pay the mortgage, utilities, taxes, and employees before I could even get a paycheck. I was one of the lowest paid people in the place, and that's not breaking down the pay for the hours worked. If I did that, it wouldn't even have been minimum wage.

I tried setting up a location to do aesthetic services after closing the business, just to be able to honor the gift cards. Of course the television news people hounded the owners and other renters so much, that I was asked to leave before I could even get licensed. I was able to take the retail products with me when I left, because they were paid for on my personal credit cards. I redeemed gift cards for anyone that contacted me for over a year and a half after closing, with products, readings, or tickets to my shows. Some people were redeeming certificates that they had held on to for ten years. Then I was called a charlatan, my abilities are nothing more than another "scam." I wonder if the people throwing the rocks were in my shoes, if they would have the courage to come forward and tell the world what they're able to do, knowing full well they'll be made a mockery of. I wonder if they would be strong enough to weather the storm of criticism, and help other people heal the way I do. Somehow I doubt it. People for some sad reason are afraid of what they don't know, and are very quick to want to harm and not help others. Because they don't have the ability, they don't believe anyone else does either. Little do they know, we all possess many of the abilities that I have, they just don't have the knowledge or desire to awaken and tap into them.

People have no idea who I am. I'm a good honest person, who always tried to do the right thing in life. Sometimes it's been a struggle, but I'm proud of whom I am, and I believe I set a good example for my children. I don't lie, cheat, or steal, and I never have. It's amazing when your world falls apart, who falls by the wayside, and who comes to rescue you. Only true friends stayed. Even my church disowned me, choosing to believe the news stations, and not wanting to be associated with me. I had to remind myself, that they're still a business. This is one of the reasons I say I am not religious, I'm spiritual. God doesn't require money, only faith. I'm not perfect, I never claimed to be. I make mistakes all the time, I'm human. I try to make the best choice that I can however, at any given time, I listen to my guides and angels for direction in my life, and I always try to take other people into consideration when making my decisions. I don't have all the answers, I don't know where my life is going, and I can't really predict my own future. (No good medium can, because we influence ourselves.) I do know, however, that whatever happens, wherever I end up, it will always be for my highest and best, I'll always be happy and grateful, and I'll always be doing God's work.

LIVING MY TRUE PATH

Never in my life could I have imagined that I'd be doing the work that I'm doing. I never knew I had such a gift, and I can't image what my skill level would be if I'd been paying attention at a younger age. They've shown me so much from the other side that sometimes I just have to do nothing and just process everything I've learned! Every time I do a reading for someone, or bring a soul through from the other side, I learn something else new. Sometimes the information coming out of my mouth is so foreign to me, that I have to write it down and figure out what they're trying to teach me later. In such a short time, I've learned so much that I can offer, to help other people. There is nothing more fulfilling, than being able to give closure to someone that needs it, or heal a wound for someone either here, or on the other side. Yes, sometimes they're still hurting over there just as much as someone over here is. It's more difficult for them, because they can't get through to you here, unless you come to someone like me that can facilitate. For that reason, I started doing large gallery readings. I didn't just want to accommodate more people. I wanted to educate them that there is life after life! Not a lot of mediums are comfortable in that arena, but for me it's almost second nature. The more people I can help, the more people I want to help.

There is so much we still don't know about the other side. As much as my soul can go back and forth sometimes, it's only for a limited time. You can't leave your body for that long, or obviously you would die. Most of the time, it's just a part of my soul that travels to the other side, the part that people call the aura.

It's interesting, as a psychic medium, everyone likes to joke about why we don't win the million dollar lottery or predict something that's going to happen for ourselves in advance. For the most part, it's because we sometimes aren't supposed to know, and it can be difficult to be impartial when you want something. We do, however, head off a lot of our own problems if we pay attention to the signs they send us and our own intuition. That's true for everyone. You need to be awake and aware in order to see what they're trying to show you.

I do teach mediumship and psychic development in a five-week series twice a year. I had mixed feelings about teaching when I started. I really didn't think I was knowledgeable enough to teach. But my guides made it very clear that it's our responsibility to pass on the knowledge that we have to others. They reminded me of what my life was like when my abilities first opened up. I was going crazy trying to find someone to explain it all to me, and teach me how to turn it on and off! Since writing my first book, I've encountered quite a few people that are in the same boat that I was in. Unfortunately, they live in areas with very few people who are able to help them. I was sending out draft copies of my book *A Night On The Other Side* before it was printed, so they could learn how to get it under control, before they were harmed by any negative attachments. For those of you that don't know, everyone has psychic abilities. If you want to learn how to improve yours, you can get the book and try some of the meditation recommendations. Every medium is a psychic, but every psychic is not a medium. I hope to start an online course to help people that don't have education in their area, in the hopes of awakening more people.

My favorite expression is "Love and Light." It's what we're meant to live in, that and abundance. I'm proof that you can overcome any adversity in your life, and thrive, not just survive in your life. Find your path, your true purpose in life, and follow it.

I leave you all with this thought to ponder; what kind of world do you want to live in? One that's over-populated, polluted, with no nutritional food to eat, no clean water to drink, and people that are always fighting each other and at war? Or do we want a world of love, joy, peace, and caring? The choice is ours as a race to decide, but it starts one person at a time. If every person awakened, made heart-centered decisions, and did their part, we may just have a chance to save the human race. Every person touches so many lives, just imagine……..

ADDENDUM

Just as I was taking the book to print, the family was able to gain access to my father's apartment. It had become the drug haven for my nephew, William Jr., after he had held my father hostage on his deathbed and ransacked everything he had left, financially or otherwise. There wasn't much left of the apartment other than trash. He had sold all the appliances, furniture, and business equipment.

In there, I came across letters and cards written to my father from a lot of the women that were in and out of his life while we were growing up. He stamped the date on everything he received. One of the women he corresponded with wasn't able to have children. He talked to her about wanting to have more, even though at that time he was sixty-one years old! I also found a picture of my aunt, my mother's sister. Apparently, he had carried it in his wallet for years, instead of a picture of my mother.

I also came across letters from my siblings, constantly begging for forgiveness and trying to obtain some sliver of love and recognition from a man that didn't have an inkling of the meaning of the word. It seems that all the children had self-esteem issues, still trying to have their father prove their self-worth even into adulthood.

My father when he was in the navy at age 19 and at age 13.

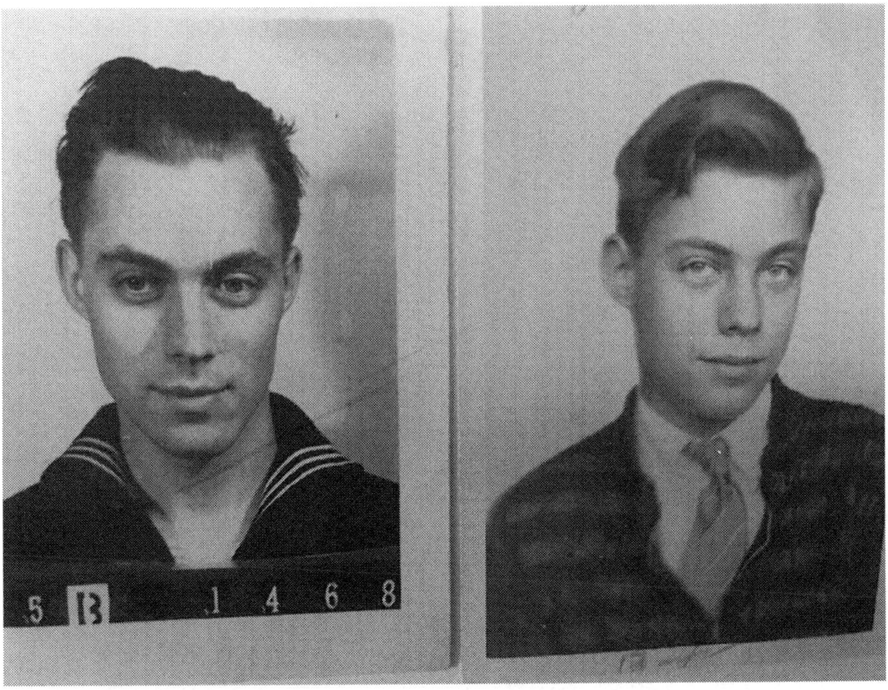

My Aunt Millie, the picture my father carried in his wallet.

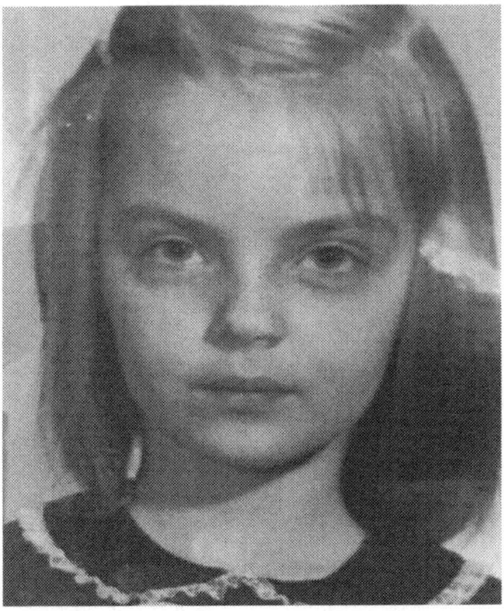

My sister Gwen, during the years she was being abused.

Albert, right before the car accident.

Millie right before she ran way with the Hare Krishna.

My mother and I, she cut all my hair off after the picture was taken.

My brother William Sr., went through the boot-camp in the Marines, and then went AWOL.

Shirley at age 13, already doing drugs.

A picture Shirley drew prior to her 15th Birthday, about smoking pot.

Contact information for June Edward "The Massachusetts Medium"

Email june@juneedward.com

Website Juneedward.com

Twitter @junemassmedium

Instagram juneedwardmassmedium

Pinterest juneedward.com

Facebook JuneEdward11

Skype june@juneedward.com

Phone 508-259-1231

I offer classes in Psychic development and Mediumship twice a year currently, and hope to be adding more classes soon. Unfortunately they are only in person in Massachusetts, and not on the internet at his time.

Imprint: Independently published
ISBN: 978-0-692-18643-5

Made in the USA
Middletown, DE
09 June 2024

55510466R00135